Women who Murder
Robert C. Jones

Robert C. Jones
POB 1775
Kennesaw, GA 30156

jone442@bellsouth.net
rcjbooks.com

"Women who Murder", Copyright 2023 by Robert C. Jones. All rights reserved.

First Edition

ISBN: 9798375423487

Table of Contents

Introduction 5
Pre-20th Century 6
   Elizabeth Báthory 6
   Lizzie Borden 12
   Amelia Dyer 22
   Delphine Lalaurie 26
   Mary Surratt 29
   Jane Toppan 40
20th/21st Century 47
   Amy Archer-Gilligan 47
   Jodi Arias 49
   Velma Barfield 51
   Arizona "Ma" Barker 52
   Juana Barraza 59
   Griselda Blanco 61
   Leonarda Cianciulli 65
   Nannie Doss 69
   Belle Gunness 73
   Gwendolyn Graham & Catherine May Wood 77
   Karla Homolka 80
   Genene Jones 82
   Manson Girls 85
      Susan Atkins 87
      Lynette ""Squeaky" Fromme 93
      Leslie Van Houten 96
      Patricia Dianne Krenwinkel 101
   Nazis 106
      Dorothea Binz 107
      Therese Rosi Brandl 108
      Irmgard Furchner 109
      Irma Grese 111
      Irmgard Huber 115

Ilsa Koch	117
Johanna Langefeld	122
Maria Mandel	124
Elisabeth Volkenrath	126
Bonnie Parker	131
Dorothea Puente	137
Aileen Wuornos	139
Andrea Yates	143
Sources	145
The Author on YouTube	148
About the Author	149

Introduction

It is often stated in the media that few women are serial killers – that it is a male manifestation. However, there are many exceptions to the rule. There are 35 female criminals discussed in this book, and most of them killed at least one person. Some killed hundreds of thousands of people (and were hung for their efforts).

Two of the people in this book didn't actually kill anyone, although they both conspired to kill the President of the United States - Mary Surratt and Lynette "Squeaky" Fromme. Lizzie Borden is included, although it should be point out that she was found not guilty of murder.

Clearly, the most horrifying of the criminals mentioned herein are the Nazis concentration camp female employees. It almost seems strange to include Jodi Arias in the same category as Nazi Maria Mandel. However, both, ultimately, were murderers.

This book grew out of a course I taught for Brenau University BULLI program during the pandemic. Hurray for Zoom!

Robert Jones
Rome, Georgia
February 2023

Pre-20th Century

Elizabeth Báthory

Date	Events
August 7, 1560	Born in Nyírbátor, Kingdom of Hungary
May 8, 1575	Marries Count Ferenc Nádasdy at the palace of Vranov nad Topľou; the couple would own land in both Transylvania and Hungry. They would have 8 children.
1578	Count Nádasdy becomes chief commander of Hungarian troops against the Ottomans; Elizabeth manages the estates
January 4, 1604	Count Ferenc Nádasdy dies
1590/1610	Elizabeth and four collaborators murder hundreds of girls. Lutheran minister István Magyari made complaints against her at the court in Vienna.
1610	György Thurzó, the Palatine of Hungary, is ordered by the Holy Roman Emperor Matthias to investigate the rumors
October 1610	52 witness statements collected
December 1610	She is imprisoned within Castle of Csejte, in present day Slovakia
1611	300 witness statements collected
January 2, 1611, January 17, 1611	Trials for Elizabeth Báthory. Evidence was primarily hearsay, with little direct evidence.
December 31, 1612	Elizabeth and four servants are arrested. Elizabeth is placed under house arrest.
1612	Detained in the castle of Csejte for the rest of her life
August 21,	Dies in her bed of unknown causes; buried in the

Date	Events
1614	church of Csejte (the location of her body today is unknown)
1729	Jesuit scholar László Turóczi's publishes *Tragica Historia*, about the Báthory case. This is the first time that the bathing in the blood of young girls' story is told.
1765	The original witness statements are published. They don't mention baths of blood.
1850	John Paget publishes *Hungary and Transylvania*; the blood bath story reappears
1970	Ingrid Pitt stars in *Countess Dracula* about Elizabeth
1991	The character "Mad" Danelle Lothston appears in George R. R. Martin novel *A Game of Thrones*; she kidnaps children, and bathes in their blood
2008	Slovakian film *Bathory* released, featuring Anna Friel
2010	Appears in the novel, *Abraham Lincoln, Vampire Hunter* (Seth Grahame-Smit)

Elizabeth Báthory was born in Nyírbátor, Kingdom of Hungary in 1560. She would go on to marry Count Ferenc Nádasdy in 1575.

From 1590/1610, Elizabeth and four collaborators murdered hundreds of girls. The would be lured into her castle, and then imprisoned in cells. It is said that torture frequently preceded death.

Somewhat ironically, the thing that everyone thinks they know about Bathory is probably apocryphal. There is no reference to her bathing in her victim's blood until 1729 – her death was over 100 years before, in 1614, in the castle of Csejte.

In 1610, György Thurzó, the Palatine of Hungary, was ordered by the Holy Roman Emperor Matthias to investigate the rumors against Bathory. On December 31, 1612, Elizabeth and four servants were arrested. Elizabeth was placed under house arrest - the four servants were executed. Bathory was to spend the rest of her life in the castle of Csejte. Some accounts said that she was confined to one room, but other accounts show that she had the run of the castle.

17th century portrait of Elizabeth Bathory[1]

Below is a newspaper account from 1894 which shows many of the "additions" to the story since the death of Bathory

---

[1] Public Domain.

SHE MURDERED FOR BEAUTY

No more remarkable criminal ever lived than the Countess Elizabeth Bathori the countess of blood a murderess, who almost unaided, deliberately killed 60 people in 6 years.

Her diabolical crimes are described in a volume now in press in a leading, publishing house in Breslau.

The Countess Elizabeth was the niece of Bathori or Bathory, king of Poland, and wife of the Hungarian Count Nadasdy. She was born in the latter half of the 16th century. The author describes her as a woman of much apparent refinement, slender in figure, delicate in appearance, educated and accomplished.

In her crimes she was aided by a manservant and two women, all of whom seem to have entered into the villainy with quite as much fervor as the mistress herself. The man was frequently employed in kidnapping young girls when it was found impossible to secure them by other means.

Upon one occasion the countess, by some breach of duty on the part of her maid, seized a toilet article with a sharp point and plunged it into the girl's neck. The blow severed the carotid artery. The blood spurted forth [on the] hands of countess and her face. This maddened her and aroused a new element in her nature. She washed her hands in the blood, and, as the girl lay prostrate on the floor, the countess lifted her feet to a chair so that the blood would more rapidly flow towards her neck.

She caught the flow in a vessel. The girl bled to death, and the countess discovered that the awful bath had made her own skin much whiter and softer than it had been before. This was the beginning of her series of murders and tortures. The count became a party to the infamy.

The diversion of the couple did not stop at murder, but included torture of the most ingenious and horrible description.

The chateau had many dangerous and passages well adapted to this cruel work. Here one night during the Christmas holidays the countess spread a royal supper and invited to it 25 young damsels from the adjacent district. The girls naturally felt honored by the attention thus shown them. The supper was sumptuous, and the tables were loaded down with rich plates. The banquet took place in a special hall underground, the better to give the guests a novel experience, as the countess blandly explained.

At the conclusion of the repast the maidens were invited one by one to inspect subterranean passages, and as they went down the corridors with their guides they were shown into different cells and the doors closed upon them. Then the work of slaughter began.

The countess, with her party, visited the various rooms. The three servants fell upon the girls and disrobed them, while the count and countess sat looking on.

"When they were thus prepared, the countess, causing the wretched maidens to be held down that they might not struggle, drew from her pocket a sharp knife and deftly cut the most sensitive nerves in the girl, then cut off bits of flesh, pierced the eyes and ended the suffering by cutting the jugular vein or plunging the knife into the heart. In each case the blood was preserved with great care.

In this manner, varying the mode of torture to suit her increasing savagery, the countess went from one cell to another until she had with her own hands killed the entire number of her guests.

One of the girls was spared until the next day, when early in the morning she was smeared over her entire body with honey and tied to a post in the midst of a swarm of wasps and there she was left for 24 hours, being in that time stung to death. The count and his wife meanwhile sat at a window near by and watched the suffering of their victim. After it was over the body was drained of its blood.

The blood gathered from these girls was at once used by the countess to bath her neck and face. Vanity had much to do with these terrible crimes, for it was in the beautifying of her complexion that the countess first found an excuse for her actions.

The love of torture grew on her with the increase of her crimes and the familiarity she acquired with suffering.

The countess caused one of her girls to be stood, nude, in a hogshead of ice water and kept there for four hours after which she was clothed in a single muslin garment soaked in ice water and then tied to the top of a tall tower, while a furious snowstorm raged, and was kept there all night. In the morning the maiden was dead,

Her washerwoman she strapped to the wall and burned out her eyes, nose and tongue with a red-hot iron, She kept the poor woman alive for several days, burning her afresh every hour and torturing her in many horrible ways.

The supply of victims failing, she directed the man, Fierko, to go out to the distant country and kidnap, induce or otherwise get victims to visit the chateau. Then the favorite plan of the countess was to have a mock ceremony of marriage performed, the man Fierko acting as bridegroom and the receiving and assurance that in marrying they would acquire their freedom the following day, whereas by refusing they would be committing suicide, inasmuch as they would in that event be killed.

A girl would be conducted to a dungeon fitted up like a royal boudoir. During the night the bride would be awakened by the countess, who would plunge a knife into her heart as soon as she opened her eyes.

A method that the countess found greatly to her liking was to have the victim suspended by ropes from the ceiling, and gently open a vein in her body and watch her slowly bleed to death.

The stories told of these murders created scandal. George Thurzo, governor of the Provence and cousin of the countess, warned his relative to cease her terrible crimes. But still murders continued, and finally even the governor made up his mind that they should be stopped by force.

Learning that his cousin had arranged for usual Christmas

wholesale killing, he took some officers and went to the chateau. He found in the cellars of the building 20 young women tied to the walls without clothes and horribly maltreated.

These girls were to be killed that same night, and elaborate preparations had been made for slaughter. The girls told the governor that they had been there for a month and that there had been many more, but that every day one was selected to be killed, and when the selection had been made the victim met her fate then and there in the presence of the others.

Each day the countess would torture them, and she showed wonderful ingenuity in her means of doing so. One girl had a bosom cut off by the countess, another had lost her ears, another her nose, and all had been 'mutilated with a devilish ferocity.

One was hanging from the wall by her arm, which bad been pierced by a great spike, and a large basin was placed on the ground in order that the blood might not be lost.

Elizabeth Bathori was arrested but owing to the fact that she was a member of the reigning house she was not condemned to death. She was imprisoned for the rest of her life in the fortress of Esej, and her death took place there on Aug. 21, 1641, after she had been locked up 31 years.

She was 54 years old at her death and died from starvation. Altogether, she had killed over 650 girls.[2]

Lizzie Borden

> Lizzie Borden took an axe
> and gave her mother forty whacks.
> When she saw what she had done,
> she gave her father forty-one.

---

[2] *The Hartford republican.* (Hartford, Ky.), November 30, 1894

Date	Events
July 19, 1860	Lizzie Andrew Borden is born in Fall River, Massachusetts
May 1892	Lizzie's father kills a number of pigeons in his barn with an axe
July 1892	Lizzie and her sister Emma take extended vacations in New Bedford following a family argument
Late July 1892	Lizzie returns to Fall River
August 4, 1892	Axe murders of Lizzie's father and stepmother (11:00 a.m.)
August 8, 1892	Inquest hearing
August 11, 1892	Lizzie presented with a warrant of arrest; she is then jailed
November 7, 1891	Grand jury convened
December 2, 1892	Lizzie is indicted
June 1, 1893	Another axe murder in Fall River; Jose Correa de Mello is convicted in 1894
June 5, 1893	Trial begins; among the prosecutors, future United States Supreme Court Justice William H. Moody; among the defenders, former Massachusetts governor George D. Robinson
June 5, 1893	The skulls are presented as evidence in the trial
June 20, 1893	Lizzie acquitted. The jury met for 1.5 hours.
1897	Accused of shoplifting in Providence, Rhode Island
1905	After the murders, Emma and Lizzie bought a house and lived together. Emma left in 1905 after an argument, and never returned.
June 1, 1927	Dies of pneumonia in Fall River, Massachusetts
June 10, 1927	Emma dies of kidney disease
1975	Portrayed by Elizabeth Montgomery in the ABC film *The Legend of Lizzie Borden*

Date	Events
2014	Portrayed by Christina Ricci in TV *movie Lizzie Borden Took an Ax*
2018	Portrayed by Chloë Sevigny in *Lizzie*

She was born Lizzie Andrew Borden in Fall River, Massachusetts on July 19, 1860. She would become one of the most famous alleged murderesses in the 19th century.

The murders occurred on August 4, 1892, at around 11:00 a.m. The father and stepmother of Lizzie Borden were both killed by axe.

Suspicion quickly turned to Lizzie Borden, as she and the maid were supposedly the only ones in the house. This was not quite true, as a cousin, John V. Morse, was said to have visited the house the morning of the murders.

On August 11, 1892, Lizzie was presented with a warrant of arrest and jailed. The trial began on June 5, 1893. The case was weak forensically, and on June 20, 1893, Lizzie was acquitted. The jury met for 1.5 hours.

One of the bits of evidence brought against Lizzie Borden was that she had tried to buy poison from the local apothecary prior to the murder. The eyewitness account was later impinged. Also, it was unclear what part poison played in the axe murders of two people.

After the trial, Lizzie's sister Emma and Lizzie bought a house and lived together. Emma left after an argument in 1905, and never returned.

Lizzie Borden died on June 1, 1927 of pneumonia in Fall River,

Massachusetts

"Andrew Borden, father of Lizzie Borden, slain in his house in Fall River. Police forensic photograph. 1892".[3]

---

[3] The Burns Archive. 1892 police photo. Public Domain.

Portrait of Lizzie Borden in 1890[4]

Below is a lengthy newspaper article that describes the murder and discusses the possible suspects. It was written before the trial of Lizzie Borden.

> The double murder of Andrew J. Borden and his wife at Fall River, Mass. on the 4th of August, culminating as it did in the arrest of his youngest daughter, Lizzie Borden, has been one of the most extraordinary and mysterious criminal episodes of the century.
>
> The circumstances surrounding the assassination of Borden and his wife, who was Lizzie's stepmother, were such as to astound those who would pounce, offhand, upon a motive. Borden was rich and pious, aged seventy-six years, a man whose probity was equal to his thrift, he had not led a public life, he had no known enemy who it could be conjectured would go to the extent of killing him, much less his wife, and when the mutilated bodies of the couple were discovered, in their own house, shortly before noon on August 4, the police and the public were utterly at a loss for motive, and in the intense excitement that overwhelmed the community they turned to one another in helpless astonishment and horror.

---

[4] *The Guardian*, 1890. Public Domain.

The body of Borden was found on a velvet sofa in the parlor of the house. His head had been literally hacked to pieces. There were seven long gashes on his face and skull, some of them an inch and half deep through the flesh and bone. In the "spare" bed chamber on the second floor was discovered the body of Mrs. Borden, who was sixty-seven years old. There was at first no sight of blood and the momentary supposition was that heart failure had occurred.

Mrs. Borden was lying prone on the floor on her face with her arms outstretched and the toes of her shoes resting on the carpet. On raising the body there was seen a pool of blood, and an examination disclosed the fact that death had been caused, as in the case of the husband, by repeated blows of some heavy sharp instrument on the face, neck and head. In the case of both there was found a deep cut into the brain.

A circumstance, which was not at once observed, but which was afterward noticed and put down as a clue, was the remarkable absence of blood from the numerous wounds on both bodies. It was as if the life current had been retarded and partly congealed from other causes before the murderous blows were struck.

A slight survey served to make it equally plain that the murders were both committed unexpectedly so far as the victims were concerned. Borden's body was reclining on the lounge, the legs were resting easily on the floor, the left arm lay on the hip, the right was folded across the breast, the eyes were closed and the features were unmarked by any expression of surprise or apprehension. The attitude was one of repose. The features of Mrs. Borden were not drawn and there was absolutely no evidence of a struggle.

There were, so far as yet known, but two persons other than Borden and his wife on the premises when the murders were committed. These were Bridget Sullivan, a domestic, and Lizzie Borden, the youngest of the two daughters. The older daughter was visiting in another town.

The first alarm was given by Lizzie Borden, who ran out into the yard and called for help. A neighbor responded and the police were telephoned for. When they arrived they were told the following story:

The elder daughter had been visiting for some time in Fair Haven. At 8 o'clock that morning Mrs. Borden received a note asking her to call on a friend who was ill. She left the house and shortly after her husband followed and went to the bank, of which he was director. He returned about 10:30 o'clock and reclined on the sofa in the parlor tor a doze. Bridget Sullivan, who had been working in the kitchen, passed through the parlor shortly after his return and asked him how he felt.

The reason for this question was explained to the police. The whole family had been slightly ill for a day or two, and Dr. Bowen, the attending physician, had given it as his suggestion that they had been poisoned. Mr. Borden told Bridget that he was feeling all right, and she went up to the third floor and washed the windows.

According to Lizzie Borden she slept late that morning, and did not get up until Mrs. Borden had gone out, as she thought, in response to the note from the neighbor. On going down stairs Lizzie passed through the parlor and saw and spoke to her father. Supposing her mother was out, she went Into the yard and entered the barn In search of a piece of lead, from which to cut "sinkers" for a fishing excursion she expected soon to make to Marion to join some Sunday school friends who were already sojourning there. While in the barn she heard a cry of distress coming apparently from the house. Rushing in, she found her father dead on the sofa. She called Bridget and they gave an alarm. Then they searched upstairs for Mrs. Borden and found her as described. The door of the spare room, the police were told, was closed.

Such was the story as related to the police by Lizzie Borden and the servant, and it furnished no clues on which to work. A search of the house revealed a hatchet which bore traces of blood, a bundle of bloody rags under a bucket in the cellar and two spots of blood on a white skirt hanging in a closet in Lizzie's room. This skirt would hardly stand as evidence, however, unless it could be proven that Lizzie wore it when she killed the stepmother, but removed it before she made the assault on the old man. She did not have time to change any of her clothing between the time Mr. Borden was killed and the time when she called Bridget Sullivan. There was absolutely no stain of blood on Lizzie's hands or clothing when the officers took possession of the house.

The first theory of the police was that a murderer familiar with the place had concealed himself in the house and had taken desperate chances for the plunder that might be at hand. This view was relinquished when it was found that nothing bad been taken. The police next turned their attention to the theory that the murders were a family matter and had grown out of the efforts of one of the girls to secure a half interest in the estate, valued at $500,000.

At the outset there were several false clues on which the police worked, several parties being arrested on suspicion, but each one established an alibi.

A careful examination of the bodies of Mr. and Mrs. Borden the day after the killing served to convince the physicians that Mrs. Borden had been dispatched some time probably an hour and a half before her husband. It was after this discovery, coupled with their failure to locate any suspicious character on or near the premises before or after the tragedy, and with the seeming improbability that a stranger could have lurked In the Borden house without detection by Lizzie Borden or the servant, that the police fell back on the theory that the assassin was some member of the household who knew the premises thoroughly.

So much having been settled to their satisfaction the police proceeded to look for their victim. Their attention was first drawn to John V. Morse, a cousin of Borden, living in a neighboring town. Morse was a sort of horse trader, had recently come from the West and was known to have been at the Borden home several times, and especially on the morning of the murders. He was shadowed and questioned by the police, and several of the Borden relatives came out and aired their suspicions in relation to him, but he convinced the police of his innocence. Morse was undoubtedly in and about the Borden house shortly before the tragedy, but there was no evidence of any sort discovered against him, and he was not arrested, although he was under surveillance for several days.

Lizzie Borden was suspected chiefly by reason of certain discrepancies between her statements to the police as to the circumstances under which the bodies of Mr. and Mrs. Borden were found. Bridgett Sullivan was involved in several of the earlier of these discrepancies, but the police decided that she was a victim of a bad memory and abandoned all suspicion of her.

The suspicion against Lizzie Borden was rendered stronger by a statement made to the police by Eli Bence, a clerk at I. H. Smith's drugstore, to the effect that Miss Borden had been in his store two days before the murders Inquiring for prussic acid or hydrocyanic acid. She failed to secure either. The drug clerk made a partial identification of Miss Borden, but later the accuracy of his identification was denied. Miss Borden denied that she bad bought or tried to buy either poison. Hydrocyanic acid leaves no outward trace on the body, and it was the conjecture of the physicians for the prosecution that this was the drug that had been used.

Miss Borden was put under police surveillance two days after the murders, but was not arrested until some days later. In addition to the police there was a Pinkerton detective early on the scene. The detective worked in the interest of the Borden family and ridiculed
the police theory. His idea was that the murders were the work of a lunatic.

The movements of Mr. Borden on the day of his death were investigated, with the result that the police were able to trace him up to within a half hour of his death. Thirty minutes after he was seen to enter the house his body was found on the sofa. It was between 10:30 and 10:52 a.m. when Borden entered the house. At 11:13 the news of the murder was on the street.

In the case of Mrs. Borden the police were utterly unable to locate her outside the house on that fearful morning, not withstanding the statement of Lizzie Borden that Mrs. Borden had been summoned to a sick neighbor. According to Miss Borden the note was delivered to Mrs. Borden by a messenger boy, but she could not describe the boy. She did not know the neighbor and diligent search failed to reveal the slightest trace of either. The note which Mrs. Borden is said to have received could not be found. It was regarded as singular by the police that neither Miss Borden nor Bridget Sullivan had heard the noise of the fall of Mrs. Borden's body. Mrs. Borden weighed 200 pounds, and it was clear that she had tumbled headlong and at full length to the floor.

Dr. Bowen, the family physician, who was called to the Borden house a few minutes after the discovery of the bodies, told the police that Mr. Borden was, in his judgment, asleep when attacked. He thought that an ax was used, as there were several cuts on the head four and a half inches long.

Miss Borden told the police that she was in the barn when the murders occurred. A policeman visited the barn on the day after the tragedy and examined the floor, which was covered with a thick layer of dust. There were no footprints in this dust except those made by the officer in his investigation.

Hiram Harrington, a brother-in-law of Borden, had an interview with Miss Borden the evening of the day of the murders. She told him that she was in the kitchen when the father came home at 10:30 o'clock. Mr. Borden sat down on the lounge in the next room, and she went in there and helped him to remove his coat, inquired solicitously as to his condition, put on his dressing gown, assisted him to a reclining position, and withdrew on finding him comfortable.

She left the house and went to the barn about 10:45 o'clock, and stayed there twenty to thirty minutes. On returning she found Mr. Borden's body. Miss Borden told Harrington that she thought the murders bad been committed by strangers.

The police were clear on the question of motive. They alleged that it was the purpose of Lizzie Borden, by killing Borden and bis wife, to inherit one-half of his estate. Before the tragedy Lizzie Borden lived the humdrum life of a small place. She once taught a Sunday school class and was bright but sedate. She made an extended tour of Europe a year or two ago, since which she has devoted herself largely to novels and has resumed her Sunday school teaching. Throughout her surveillance and arrest she acted with wonderful calm..[5]

"The Borden murder trial—A scene in the court-room before the acquittal - Lizzie Borden, the accused, and her counsel, Ex-Governor Robinson"[6]

Amelia Dyer

Date	Events
1834	*Poor Law Amendment Act* passed, removing financial obligation from unwed fathers
1837	Born Amelia Elizabeth Hobley at Pyle Marsh, Bristol, England

---

[5] *Washington Star*, 1893.
[6] *Frank Leslie's illustrated newspaper*, v. 76 (1893 June 29)

Date	Events
c. 1861	Marries George Thomas (d. 1869)
1872	Marries William Dyer; they will have two children
1879	Sentenced to hard labor for six months because of some suspicions about her childcare practices
1884	National Society for the Prevention of Cruelty to Children formed
1890	Feigns insanity when a governess who left a child in her care becomes suspicious
1893	Discharged from the Somerset and Bath Lunatic Asylum; Amelia had been in and out of lunatic asylums most of her life
January 1896	Barmaid Evelina Marmon has an illegitimate child she names Doris; she hands her over for adoption to Amelia Dyer along with 10 pounds.
March 30, 1896	• Amelia murders Doris Marmon by wrapping tape around the baby's neck • A bargeman retrieves a package from the Thames containing the body of Helena Fry
April 1, 1896	Amelia murders Harry Simmons using the same tape she killed Doris Marmon with
April 2, 1896	Stuffs the results of her most recent murders into carpetbags, and tosses them into the Thames
April 3, 1896	Police raid her home
April 4, 1896	Arrested for murder; consequently, 6 more bodies were found in the Thames with tape around their necks
April 16, 1896	Amelia writes her confession
May 22, 1896	Found guilty of the death of Doris Marmon
June 10, 1896	Hanged at Newgate Prison, London at 9:00 a.m.

Amelia Dyer was born in 1837 as Amelia Elizabeth Hobley at

Pyle Marsh, Bristol, England. She had a long history of mental illness and spent time in and out of insane asylums over the years.

She was a practitioner of the practice of *baby farming* – she took in infants no one else wanted. The catch here is that she charged a fee to take the children in.

As early as 1879, there were questions about her childcare practices. She was sentenced to hard labor for six months because of some suspicions about her childcare practices.

Over a 20-year period, it is thought that she murdered over 400 children. She would receive payment for taking care of an infant, and then murder the child so that she didn't have to care for or feed the child.

Things went along nicely for her little business until January 1896. A barmaid named Evelina Marmon had an illegitimate child she named Doris. Evelina handed Doris over for adoption to Amelia Dyer, along with 10 pounds in cash.

On March 30, 1896, Amelia murdered Doris Marmon by strangling her by wrapping white tape around the baby's neck. Her typical procedure was to strangle the child, and then stuff them into a carpet bag and toss it into the Thames. Unfortunately for Amelia, a bargeman retrieved a package from the Thames containing the body of one Helena Fry – another victim of Amelia Dyer.

On April 1, 1896, Amelia murdered Harry Simmons using the same tape she killed Doris Marmon with. The next day she stuffed Harry and other recent victims into bags and tossed them into the Thames.

On April 3, 1896, the police raided her home, partly because Evelina Marmon couldn't get a straight answer from Dyer on how her (now dead) child was fairing. On April 4, 1896, Amelia was arrested for murder; consequently, 6 more bodies were found in the Thames with tape around their necks. Amelia fessed up to the murders on April 16, 1896. On May 22, 1896, she was found guilty of the death of Doris Marmon. Amelia was hanged at Newgate Prison, London at 9:00 a.m. on June 10, 1896.

The killing rampage had ended.

Amelia Dyer[7]

7

Delphine Lalaurie

Date	Events
March 19, 1787	Born Marie Delphine Macarty in New Orleans, Spanish Louisiana
June 11, 1800	Marries Don Ramón de Lopez y Angulo in New Orleans (d. 1804); they would have one child
June 1808	Marries Jean Blanque (d. 1816); they would have 4 children
June 25, 1825	Marries Leonard Louis Nicolas LaLaurie
November 16, 1832	Leonard and Delphine separated
1831/34	Slaves are mistreated at her house at 1140 Royal Street; 12 slaves die. In time, mobs burn the house to the ground. The slaves are taken to the local jail.
April 10, 1834	After a fire occurs in her mansion, responders discover bound slaves in her attic that have been tortured
1834	Delphine Lalaurie flees to Paris
December 7, 1849	Dies in Paris, France

Delphine Lalaurie[8]

---

[8] Public Domain.

Delphine LaLaurie was born as Marie Delphine Macarty on March 19, 1787 in New Orleans, Spanish Louisiana. From 1831/34, slaves were tortured at her house at 1140 Royal Street. At least 12 slaves died. On April 10, 1834, after a fire occurred in her mansion, responders discovered bound slaves in her attic that had been tortured. Delphine escaped justice by fleeing to Paris. Below are two accounts written about the situation, the first written in 1838, and the second in 1890.

> A horrible sight met their eyes. Of the nine slaves, the skeletons of two were afterwards found poked into the ground; the other seven could scarcely be recognised as human. Their faces had the wildness of famine, and their bones were coming through the skin. They were chained and tied in constrained postures; some on their knees, some with their hands above their heads. They had iron collars with spikes which kept their heads in one position. The cowhide, stiff with blood, hung against the wall; and there was a step-ladder on which this fiend stood while flogging her victims, in order to lay on the lashes with more effect. Every morning, it was her first employment after breakfast to lock herself in with her captives, and flog them till her strength failed.
>
> Amidst shouts and groans, the sufferers were brought out into the air and light. Food was given them,—with too much haste; for two of them died in the course of the day. The rest, maimed and helpless, are pensioners of the city.[9]

> They bring out two negresses. One has a large heavy iron collar at the neck and heavy irons on her feet. The fire is subdued now, they say, but the search goes on. Here is M. Guillotte; he has found another victim in another room. They push aside a mosquito-net and see a negro woman, aged, helpless, and with a deep wound in the head.
>
> Some of the young men lift her and carry her out...

---

[9] *Retrospect of Western Travel, Volume 2*, by Harriet Martineau (London: Saunders & Otley, 1838)

The search went on. The victims were led or carried out. The sight that met the public eye made the crowd literally groan with horror and shout with indignation. "We saw," wrote the editor of the "Advertiser" next day, "one of these miserable beings. The sight was so horrible that we could scarce look upon it. The most savage heart could not have witnessed the spectacle unmoved. He had a large hole in his head; his body from head to foot was covered with scars and filled with worms! The sight inspired us with so much horror that even at the moment of writing this article we shudder from its effects. Those who have seen the others represent them to be in a similar condition." One after another, seven dark human forms were brought forth, gaunt and wild-eyed with famine and loaded with irons, having been found chained and tied in attitudes in which they had been kept so long that they were crippled for life.

It must have been in the first rush of the inside throng to follow these sufferers into the open air and sunlight that the quick-witted Madame Lalaurie clapped to the doors of her house with only herself and her daughters—possibly the coachman also—inside, and nothing but locks and bars to defend her from the rage of the populace. The streets under her windows—Royal street here, Hospital yonder—and the yard were thronged. Something by and by put some one in mind to look for buried bodies. There had been nine slaves besides the coachman; where were the other two? A little digging brought their skeletons to light—an adult's out of the soil, and the little child's out of the "condemned well"; there they lay. But the living seven—the indiscreet crowd brought them food and drink in fatal abundance, and before the day was done two more were dead. The others were tenderly carried—shall we say it?—to prison;—to the calaboose. Thither "at least two thousand people" flocked that day to see, if they might, these wretched sufferers.[10]

---

[10] *Strange True Stories of Louisiana* by George W. Cable, Illustrated, 1890

Mary Surratt

Date	Events
c. 1823	Born near Waterloo, Maryland
November 25, 1835	Begins attending the Academy for Young Ladies in Alexandria, Virginia
August 1840	Marries John Harrison Surratt (d. 1862)
April 1844	John Surratt Jr. is born
1853	John Sr. builds a tavern and later a hotel in what would later be called Surrattsville
July 1861	John Jr. becomes a courier for the Confederacy
Late 1861	Lafayette Baker and 300 soldiers occupy Surrattsville, because of rumors of spy activity there
November 17, 1863	John Jr. is dismissed as postmaster of Surrattsville because of suspicions of disloyalty
December 1, 1864	Overwhelmed by debt, Mary moves to a townhouse in nearby Washington, D.C.; she leases the Surrattsville tavern to John M. Lloyd
November 1, 1864	Louis J. Weichmann becomes a boarder in the Surratt boardinghouse
January 1865	John Jr. transfers all of his property to his mother's name (traitor's property can be seized); over the next several months, almost all of the Lincoln assassination conspirators visit the Surratt townhouse
December 23, 1864	Samuel Mudd introduces John Jr. to John Wilkes Booth; Booth starts visiting the townhouse
April 14, 1865	• Booth visits Mary Surratt at her boarding house in Washington, and asks that she deliver a package to her tavern in Surrattsville, Maryland • Surratt complies, and delivers the package to Surrattsvile. She travels with a boarder, Louis J.

Date	Events
	Weichmann, who will later condemn her in court. • Assassination of Abraham Lincoln at Ford's Theater
April 17, 1865	Federal soldiers search the townhouse, and arrest Mary Surratt and Louis J. Weichmann; Mary is briefly incarcerated at the Old Capitol Prison
April 30, 1865	Transferred to the Washington Arsenal[11]
May 9, 1865 - June 28, 1865	The trial for the Lincoln Assassination conspirators; The charge against Mary is that she did "receive, entertain, harbor, and conceal, aid and assist" her co-defendants
July 5, 1865	Mary Surratt is found guilty
July 7, 1865	Mary Surratt is hung (and buried) at the Washington Arsenal
February 9, 1869	Mary is re-interred by the family in Mount Olivet Cemetery in Washington
2010	Robin Wright portrays Mary Surratt in *The Conspirator*

The most controversial member of the Lincoln Conspiracy put on trial at the military tribunal was Mary Surratt, mother of John Surratt. One can argue as to whether she deserved the death sentence or not (probably not), but the charge against her was that she had conspired to "receive, entertain, harbor, and conceal, aid and assist" her co-defendants, and in this it seems fairly clear that she was guilty.

---

[11] Now Fort Lesley J. McNair

The Lincoln Conspirators, with Mary Surratt in the middle[12]

---

[12] *The Assassination of President Lincoln and the Trial of the Conspirators* (Moore, Wilstach and Baldwin, 1865)

Maery Surratt[13]

There is no question that the Surratt family were Southern sympathizers. Son Isaac joined the Confederate Army in Texas in 1861. Son John Jr. acted as a courier and possibly a spy for the Confederacy. As early in the War as late 1861, Lafayette Baker was suspicious enough of the pro-secession activities in Surrattsville to show up with 300 soldiers to investigate.

At the boarding house in Washington, where Mary Surratt lived from October 1, 1864 to her death, almost all of the Lincoln conspirators either boarded or visited there, including

---

[13] National Archives and Records Administration, (NAID) 525346

Louis J. Weichmann, George Atzerodt, Lewis Powell, David Herold and John Wilkes Booth. There is no question that elements of the Lincoln assassination were hatched at the boarding house, owned and operated by Mary Surratt.

Lafayette Baker, head of the Union secret service, discussed Surrattsville and the role of the Surratt family as Confederate sympathizers in his book *History of the United States Secret Service:*

> The country immediately outside of the District of Columbia, to the south, is named Prince George's, and the pleasantest village of this county, close to Washington, is called Surrattsville. This consists of a few cabins at a crossroad, surrounding a fine old hotel, the master whereof, giving the settlement his name, left the property to his wife, who for a long time carried it on with indifferent success. Having a son and several daughters, she moved to Washington soon after the beginning of the war, and left the tavern to a trusty friend—one John Lloyd. Surrattsville has gained nothing in patronage or business from the war, except that it became, at an early date, a rebel post-office. The great secret mail from Matthias Creek, Virginia, to Port Tobacco, struck Surrattsville, and thence headed off to the east of Washington, going meanderingly north. Of this post route Mrs. Surratt was a manageress; and John Lloyd, when he rented her hotel, assumed the responsibility of looking out for the mail, as well as the duty of making Mrs. Surratt at home when she chose to visit him.

"Surrattsville, the Home of John H. Surratt"[14]

So Surrattsville, only ten miles from Washington, has been throughout the war a seat of conspiracy. It was like a suburb of Richmond, reaching quite up to the rival capital; and though the few Unionists on the peninsula knew its reputation well enough, nothing of the sort came out until after the murder.

Treason never found a better agent than Mrs. Surratt. She was a large, masculine, self-possessed female, mistress of her house, and as lithe a rebel as Belle Boyd or Mrs. Greensborough[15]. She had not the flippancy and menace of the first, nor the social power of the second; but the rebellion has found no fitter agent.

At her country tavern and Washington home, Booth was made welcome, and there began the muttered murder against the nation and mankind.

The acquaintance of Mrs. Surratt in Lower Maryland undoubtedly suggested to Booth the route of escape, and made him known to his subsequent accomplices. Last fall he visited the entire region, as far as Leonardstown, in St. Mary's County, professing to buy land, but really making himself informed upon the rebel post stations, with all the leading affiliations upon whom he could depend. At this time he bought a map, a fellow to which I have seen among Atzeroth's effects, published at Buffalo for the rebel government, and marking at haphazard all the Maryland villages,

---

[14] Library of Congress http://www.loc.gov/pictures/item/2004677307/
[15] Probably Rose Greenhow

but without tracing the high-roads at all. The absence of these roads, it will be seen hereafter, very nearly misled Booth during his crippled flight.

When Booth cast around him for assistants, he naturally selected those men whom he could control. The first that recommended himself was one Harold, a youth of inane and plastic character, carried away by the example of an actor, and full of execrable quotations, going to show that that he was an imitator of the master spirit, both in text and admiration. This Harold was a gunner, and therefore versed in arms; he had traversed the whole lower portion of Maryland, and was therefore a geographer as well as a tool. His friends lived at every farm-house between Washington and Leonardsville, and he was respectably enough connected, so as to make his association creditable as well as useful.

Young Surratt[16] does not appear to have been a puissant spirit in the scheme; indeed, all design and influence therein was absorbed by Mrs. Surratt and Booth. The latter was the head and heart of the plot; Mrs. Surratt was his anchor, and the rest of the boys were disciples to Iscariot and Jezebel. John Surratt, a youth of strong Southern physiognomy, beardless and lanky, knew of the murder and connived at it. 'Sam' Arnold and one McLaughlin were to have been parties to it, but backed out in the end. They all relied upon Mrs. Surratt, and took their 'cues' from Wilkes Booth.[17]

CHARGES

And in further prosecution of said conspiracy, Mary E. Surratt did, at Washington City, and within the military department and military lines aforesaid, on or before the 6th day of March, A. D. 1865, and on divers other days and times between that day and the 20th day of April, A. D. 1865, **receive, entertain, harbor, and conceal, aid and assist the said John Wilkes Booth, David E. Herold, Lewis Payne, John H. Surratt, Michael O'Laughlin, George**

---

[16] John Surratt Jr.
[17] *History of the United States Secret Service*, by General L.C. Baker (L.C. Baker, 1867)

> **A. Atzerodt, Samuel Arnold, and their confederates**, with the knowledge of the murderous and traitorous conspiracy aforesaid, and with intent to aid, abet, and assist them in the execution thereof, and in escaping from justice after the murder of the said Abraham Lincoln, as aforesaid. (**emphasis added**)[18]

> VERDICT
>
> Mrs. Mary E. Surratt.
>
> After mature consideration of the evidence adduced in the case of the accused, Mary E. Surratt, the Commission find the said accused—
>
> Of the Specification Guilty.
>
> Except as to "receiving, sustaining, harboring, and concealing Samuel Arnold and Michael O'Laughlin," and except as to "combining, confederating, and conspiring with Edward Spangler" of this Not Guilty.
>
> Of the Charge Guilty.
>
> Except as to "combining, confederating, and conspiring with Edward Spangler" of this Not Guilty.
>
> **And the Commission do, therefore, sentence her, the said Mary E. Surratt, to be hanged by the neck until she be dead, at such time and place as the President of the United States shall direct; two-thirds of the members of the Commission concurring therein.** (**emphasis added**)[19]

President Andrew Johnson approved of the verdict rendered against Mary Surratt and specified when the hanging should take place:

---

[18] *The Assassination of President Lincoln and the Trial of the Conspirators* (Moore, Wilstach and Baldwin, 1865)

[19] *Ibid*

Executive Mansion, July 5, 1865.

The foregoing sentences in the cases of David E. Herold, G. A. Atzerodt, Lewis Payne, and Mary E. Surratt, are hereby approved; and it is ordered, that the sentences in the cases of David E. Herold, G. A. Atzerodt, Lewis Payne, and Mary E. Surratt, be carried into execution by the proper military authority, under the direction of the Secretary of War, on the 7th day of July, 1865, between the hours of 10 o'clock, A. M., and 2 o'clock, P. M., of that day.

(Signed) ANDREW JOHNSON[20]

The New York Herald of July 8, 1865, ran a sketch of the life of Mary Surratt:

> Mrs. Surratt, nee Mary E. Jenkins, was born in the spring of 1820, and at an early age was destined for a conventual life by her parents, whose Catholic piety seemed Italian and medieval in its strictness and fervor. She was sent at the age of ten to the Catholic Seminary at Alexandria. The home of her parents, E. and Mary Jenkins, was but two miles and a half from the bridge at the Navy Yard—the bridge over which Booth was destined to enter upon his wild night ride. Twenty-one years ago Mary E. Jenkins was married to John H. Surratt, a farmer and mail station keeper of her own county and neighborhood. John did not possess much of a fervid feeling of devotion or of the exalted and intense passions of his wife. He was a simple, hard-working farmer, who thought more of the prospects of a fine harvest than of the prospects of the Church or of the coming crisis. He had few accomplishments, nor had the woman he married, outside of a somewhat extended reading of those belles letters which have had the sanction of her Church. She neither sang nor played, nor drew, seldom embroidered, and then awkwardly. On the tenets and observances of her church she could talk long and talk well, and rather chose such topics. Her eldest child was John Surratt, on whose head a price has been fixed, at whose heels are ever the ceaseless feet of the death pursuit. Hunted, homeless, fatherless, and now motherless, his sister is heart broken, John's punishment

---

[20] *Ibid*

exceeds that of any of his companions in the crime for which they have been sentenced. The mother had destined him for the church, towards whose cloisters her heart had once turned, and, like herself, he had received a strictly Catholic education; and his life and hers certainly seem to have been free from those vices which generally prepare the mind for the contemplation of crime.

The witness Weichman, whose _____ intimacy with the family was latterly greater than that of any other individual, speaks ever respectfully of Mrs. Surratt, and it is remarkable in how different a tone he would mention any of that family from that he used when speaking of any of the other accused. The family seems to have been rather reticent and retired when in Maryland. Hospitable as John Surratt, the father, was, something of a more serious and collected calm which enveloped the mother rather chilled than invited the intimacies that are generally so natural and pleasant a relief to country monotony. When her husband died, and the station and tavern had been sold and the house on H Street occupied, a very perceptible change was observed in the manners of Mrs. Surratt. Visitors whom her fastidiousness and her son's taste would have shrunk from were frequently seen at the house and in close intimacy with John. The exacting letter and protecting commands of the Church were loss religiously hooded, though the attendance was just as regular. The stage, so long the abomination of the Catholic church, at last furnished, in its gayest, most accomplished and gifted roué, the favored friend of the family. John visited the theatre as though the ritual had never forbidden it, and the mother is not known to have objected. Indeed, she becomes exceedingly intimate with Booth, and fell under his influence to an extent which has been her ruin. Certain it now is that J.W. Booth became the real master of the widowed Mary E. Surratt and the controller of all pertaining to her. The result of that intimacy is now plain to all.

The husband, John Surratt, died in 1864 of apoplexy. He was a well-to-do farmer, living about ten miles from Washington. He added to his business as a farmer the office of postmaster of his village and kept in addition a large country store. Mrs. Surratt seems to have been his chief helper in his business, his son, John H. Surratt, being a wild and reckless youth, employed at the time of his father's death in the conspiracy for which his mother was yesterday executed. Engaged in these active pursuits Mrs. Surratt, who was naturally a woman of strong mind and nerves, appears to have gradually contracted a habit of decision not characteristic of or common with her sex. She appears to have been masculine not only in person and manners, but mind; and throughout every detail of the conspiracy she appears as stolid and determined as Payne and as desperate and dramatic as Booth. Her control over her nerves, her extraordinary self-possession and her reserve indicated thoroughly her masculine character, and prepare us for the description which we have of her person. Her forty-five years had not served to counteract the effect on her person of her active disposition and habits, and the full, rounded, Amazonian-figure was not the least faded. Her face was full, and if her dull gray eyes had had aught of warmth in them would have given her the look of a well preserved voluptuary. But the gray eyes were cold and lifeless and added to the masculinity of her appearance. They were seldom lit up by excitement or pleasure, though occasionally they gleamed with a furious or stealthy glare which indexed the bad passions of her soul.

For a year or two previous to the murder of Mr. Lincoln Mrs. Surratt had been engaged in the active management of a blockade running system, by which surreptitious communication was kept up between Richmond and Washington. Her son, John H. Surratt, appears to have been the chief agent or messenger by which this was done. In planning the escape of Booth she appears to have made the trip from Washington to Dr. Mudd's residence for this purpose. Every detail was made with a care and coolness which still further illustrates the masculine character of the woman, and still further robs her of that sympathy which it is so natural to extend to one of her sex similarly situated. Her guilt was beyond question, and her whole course has been so coolly and systematically planned that it is impossible to doubt that she was willingly and knowingly an accessory to the murder of the President.[21]

One last note. It is a bit hard today to figure out what Mary Surratt really looked like. There are few pictures, and they are

---

[21] *New York Herald*, July 7, 1865

not of high-quality. Depending on the source, she is described as anything from "voluptuous" to "matronly". I only bring up the question because of all the attention that Louis Weichmann seemed to pay to her when he was her boarder (Weichman passed it off that he was just helping out the mother of an absentee son, John Surratt, Jr.) But if the real Mary Surratt was closer to the former description than the latter, that might explain Weichmann's interest.

Jane Toppan

> Her goal was to "have killed more people – helpless people – than any other man or woman who ever lived." Jane Toppan

Date	Events
March 31, 1854	Born Honora Kelley in Boston, Massachusetts
1860	Her crazy father drops her off at the Boston Female Asylum, and never sees her again
November 1862	Placed as an indentured servant in the home of Mrs. Ann C. Toppan of Lowell, Massachusetts
1885	Attends the nursing program at Cambridge Hospital; begins killing elderly patients with morphine and atropine
1885/1902	Employed as a nurse
1889	Continues her killing at Massachusetts General Hospital; she is fired the following year
1895	Kills her landlord and his wife
1899	Kills her foster sister Elizabeth with a dose of strychnine
1901	Kills Alden Davis, his wife, his sister and two of his daughters. A toxicology exam is conducted on one

Date	Events
	of the daughters, and poison is found
October 29, 1901	Arrested, and eventually confesses to 31 murders
June 23, 1902	In Barnstable County Courthouse, she is found not guilty by reason of insanity and committed for life in the Taunton Insane Hospital
August 22, 1938	Dies in the Taunton Insane Hospital

Serial killer Jane Toppan (1854-1938)[22]

She was born Honora Kelley in Boston, Massachusetts on March 31, 1854. In 1860, her crazy father dropped her off at the Boston Female Asylum, and never saw her again. She became Jane Toppan when she was placed as an indentured

---

[22] Public Domain.

servant in the home of Mrs. Ann C. Toppan of Lowell, Massachusetts in 1862.

It is thought that she murdered up to 100 people, mostly hospital and nursing patients. She later confessed to killing 31.

She began her nursing career in 1885 when she attended the nursing program at Cambridge Hospital. It is thought that she began her killing spree there, killing elderly patients with morphine and atropine.

In 1889, she continued her killing at Massachusetts General Hospital. She was fired the following year after suspicions surfaced about her patient care.

In 1895, she killed her landlord and his wife. In 1899, she killed her foster sister Elizabeth with a dose of strychnine.

The law started to close in on her in 1901 when she killed Alden Davis, his wife, his sister and two of his daughters. A toxicology exam was conducted on one of the daughters, and poison was found. She was arrested on October 29, 1901, and eventually confessed to 31 murders.

On June 23, 1902, in the Barnstable County Courthouse, she was found not guilty by reason of insanity and committed for life in the Taunton Insane Hospital. She died there on August 22, 1938.

Below are two newspaper articles that discuss the case. The first is from the *Los Angeles Herald* in November 1904, and the second is from the *Indianapolis Journal* in June of 1902.

> ... her mental delusions are frequent, almost constant, and were anyone outside to see her there would be no doubt of the

appropriateness of her incarceration. She has abandoned the careless, cheerful frame of mind in which she has heretofore been and is now fretful, peevish, even ugly, fault-finding, fearful of eating because of suspected poison, complaining of her treatment, morose—everything but remorseful. Yet when she became a nurse she developed qualities which made her agreeable, even loved, and when she was arrested some of her former patients evinced far more concern than she herself. Indeed, from the day of her arrest Jane Toppan has never shown fear of consequences, much less remorse for her murders. Poison had become a habit of her life she told the examining physicians. In planning and carrying out her homicidal acts she was, she asserted, always calm and clear-headed. After administering the poisons she experienced great relief and went to bed and slept soundly. In telling of her crimes she exhibited no bravado, but showed that she had no appreciation of the enormity of her acts...

In their report to the district attorney, upon which the court committed the woman to the hospital, the physicians said: "The salient features of the case which indicated more especially irresponsibility were: Lack of moral understanding, of natural feelings and of the ordinary motives for conduct, including criminal acts; also the general absence in her of sufficient self-control to restrain her from crime, and her disregard of consequences as shown, for example, in continuing to poison patients in full knowledge that her guilt in other recent cases was suspected; by her desire to confess her guilt at the outset, her indifference to her fate, etc. These facts seemed to us to evidence her Inability both to help doing what she did and to be affected by punishment, conditions which are the best tests of accountability." Jane Toppan is now 45 years old. Not much has been ascertained of her earliest life; but it is known that she and her sister were placed in a foundling hospital by their father, an eccentric man who drank freely. The sister is a respectable and capable woman. A younger sister Is a chronically insane patient. A third sister lead a dissolute life and is dead... It is thus evident that her taint is inborn. Once she told Dr. Stedman: "I seem to have a sort of paralysis of thought and reason. Something comes over me; I don't know what It is. I have an uncontrollable desire to give poison without regard to the consequences." All her poisoning was done with opium, with a fatal dose of atropine, and the draught was so given in Hunyadi water as to be unsuspected by the patient and by physicians as well.[23]

BOSTON. June 24. Suspected of the death of eleven persons, but indicted for murdering only three. Miss Jane Toppan. who was yesterday declared Insane, has confessed that she has killed during her career as a professional nurse no less than thirty-one human beings. This statement was made to Judge Blxby, of Stockton, senior counsel at the trial at Barnstable yesterday, when Miss Toppan was found not guilty, by reason of insanity, on the charge of murdering Mrs. Mary D. Dibbs. Judge Blxby also said Miss Toppan had admitted she had set fires and committed other serious acts. She said she could not help committing the crimes. She said she was not Insane. She said she knew she was doing wrong when she administered poisons to her victims, and she asked Judge Blxby how, under such circumstances, she could be of unsound mind. Morphine was Miss Toppan's agency for producing death. Many of her victims were unsuspecting and most intimate friends; others were the patients of reputable physicians who employed her on account of her ability as a nurse. Miss Toppan was so expert in her knowledge of how to employ drugs and poisons that she was able to escape detection for years. In the detailed story, as told to Judge Blxby, Miss Toppan did not enumerate her many victims, although she did admit the killing of Mrs. Gibbs, Mrs. Harry Gordon, of Chicago, and Alden P. Davla, all of whom died at Cataumet last summer. Miss Toppan was indicted last December for these three murders. Miss Toppan was taken to the Taunton Insane Hospital to-day to begin her life sentence.

The opinion expressed by many persons Is that Jane Toppan is a degenerate. Her case Is one of extraordinary circumstances. A nurse by profession, enjoying the confidence of an unlimited acquaintance, of seeming lovable disposition, skilled in the uses of medicine, especially of narcotics, she was at heart a maniac, whose delight at times was to see her patients writhing in death's agony. And her work did not stop there for, having baffled medical skill so that the attending physician would assign a natural cause of death, she would seem to recover her normal

---

[23] *Los Angeles Herald*, Volume XXXII, Number 36, 6 November 1904

mental poise and sorrow with the living for the loss of a loved one.

Jane Toppan's crimes were revolting beyond all description, but the details, perhaps, will never be known, for the lips of her counsel are sealed. Her confession was not made as a story of wholesale murder, but has been drawn out little by little from time to time when her counsel have talked with her in Barnstable Jail.

To the commonwealth's officers, upon whom fell the burden of prosecuting her for murder, the terrible nature of her crime was known, and step by step they followed her movements as she had nursed, not to health, but to the grave, members of families into which she had admission as a friend and companion. The case against her rested on the testimony of alienists, who not only pronounced Jane Toppan insane, but to be a degenerate. They said her impulses irresistibly compelled her to murder her patients in order that she might enjoy the sight of their struggles.

The remarkable incident in connection with the list of persons she Is said to have killed is that when it was made up she repeated with a show of interest the names of her victims, checking off the number on her finger tips. She had spoken of the deaths of Mrs. O. A. Brigham," of Lowell, a life-long friend, being the daughter of Mrs. Toppan, who took Jane from a foundling hospital In Boston, where she had borne the name of Kelly; of Mrs. Edna H. Bannister, sister to Mrs. Brigham; Miss Florence N. Calkins, housekeeper for the Bingham family; Miss Myra Conners, of the Episcopal Theological School in Cambridge. who secured for her a position in the institution; of Mrs. McNear, of Watertown, and friend; of Mr. and Mrs. Israel P. Dunham, of Cambridge. She told how she killed each, saying she used morphine and atropine mixed in mineral water and whisky. Some times she used injections, as in the case of the deaths at Cataumet. She did not remember how each individual was killed, but where they were poisoned the drugs were those mentioned.

To the alienists, to whom she made a confession of the Cataumet cases, she spoke without reserve, describing deliberately the most Indelicate details, believing that it was knowledge due to them as physicians. She said the paroxysms of desire were Intermittent and there were times when patients were quietly dying that her better nature would become uppermost and she would try to check approaching death. She might nurse the patient ever so carefully and seek to effect a cure. Then would come a craving to administer poison, and this amounted to the strongest uncontrollable impulse, which only physical restraint would stop, and then she would render her patient unconscious. In the presence of death she would gleefully fondle the patient, stare into the eyes as if it were to see the inner workings of the soul, do all possible to intensify the agony of the patients and then when the end came she would become herself again.

The alienists, listening with wonder to the story, were forced to study Jane Toppan as a subject. They found that she embodied the worst type of degeneracy, and with this clear there was no doubt of her mental condition. While murder was Jane Toppan's greatest crime, there were many lesser forms of mental depravity each in themselves deplorable. She told of setting fires in homes in which she was a nurse or visitor and intimate acquaintances tell of peculations of money and jewelry. With the money she earned, or obtained one way or another, she was in the habit of making lavish presents to her friends.

She believes that she Is not of unsound mind. This is a trait of those whose mind have become unbalanced, but in her case it is a singularity. When her counsel on hearing her story of crime exclaimed: "Jane Toppan. you must be insane." she replied: "Insane, how can I be insane? When I killed those people I knew that I was doing wrong. I was perfectly conscious that I was not doing right. I never at any time failed to realize what I was doing. Insanity is complete lack of mental responsibility, isn't it?"[24]

---

[24] *Indianapolis Journal*, Indianapolis, Marion County, 25 June 1902

20th/21st Century

Amy Archer-Gilligan

OLD FOLKS' HOME A MURDER FACTORY?

Headline in *Seattle Star*, May 10, 1916

Date	Events
October 31, 1873	Born Amy E. Duggan in Milton, Connecticut,
1890	Attends New Britain Normal School
1897	Marries James Archer
1900s	Runs a nursing home in Connecticut
1907	Archers moved to Windsor, Connecticut, and open the *Archer Home for the Elderly and Infirm*
1907/17	60 deaths in the Archer Home for the Elderly and Infirm; Franklin R. Andrews, otherwise healthy, dies suddenly after giving Amy money.
1910	James Archer dies of kidney disease
1913	Marries Michael W. Gilligan; he dies three months later of "acute bilious attack". It appears that Amy forged the will, which left everything to her.
May 1916	Nellie Pierce, sister of Franklin R. Andrews, takes the story of his brother to the *Hartford Courant*. The *Courant* publishes a series of articles under the nomenclature the *Murder Factory*. The police begin an investigation.
	The police exhume three bodies, and discover that they were all killed by poison
May 8, 1916	Amy is arrested on five counts of murder, including

Date	Events
	her dead second husband
June 18, 1917	Amy is found guilty on one count of murder, and is sentenced to death
1917	Sentenced to prison, but was later transferred to a psychiatric hospital
1919	New trial – still found guilty of a single count of murder (July 1, 1919)
1924	Transferred to *Connecticut Hospital for the Insane*
1939	Basis for *Arsenic and Old Lace*
April 23, 1962	Dies in Middletown, Connecticut

The press referred to her boarding house for old folks as the "murder factory". Between 48/60 people were murdered there by one Amy Archer-Gilligan. She was born on October 31, 1873 as Amy E. Duggan in Milton, Connecticut.

Her scam was to take in the elderly and infirm, get them to sign over their belongings to her in their wills, and then murder them. Her favorite method of killing was using arsenic. Sometimes, she had her murder-victims to-be purchase the arsenic so it wouldn't seem like she was buying large amounts of it herself.

The police launched an investigation of Archer-Gilligan after a 1916 expose in the *Hartford Courant*. Archer-Gilligan was eventually arrested on the charge of murder, and on June 18, 1917, she was found guilty on one count of murder, and was sentenced to death.

In 1919, she had a new trial, which still found her guilty of a single count of murder. In 1924, she was transferred to the Connecticut Hospital for the Insane, where she remained until her death in 1962.

She is probably most famous for being the basis for *Arsenic and Old Lace*.

Jodi Arias

Date	Events
July 9, 1980	Born in Salinas, California
September 2006	Meets Travis Alexander in Las Vegas
November 26, 2006	Jodi becomes a Mormon, which is the faith of Travis Alexander
February 2007	Starts dating Travis Alexander

Date	Events
April 2008	Travis ditches Jodi to take another woman to Cancun, scheduled for June 15, 2008
May 28, 2008	Robbery at the domicile of Jodi Arias (her grandparents); a .25 handgun is taken
June 4, 2008	Murders ex-boyfriend Travis Victor Alexander in Mesa by 27 knife wounds and a gunshot wound. Photos of Arias and Alexander are found on a camera at the scene.
July 9, 2008	Jury indicts Jodi Arias for first-degree murder in in Maricopa County, Arizona
September 11, 2008	Jodi pleads not guilty
May 8, 2013	Convicted of first-degree murder
June 22, 2013	Portrayed by Tania Raymonde in TV movie *Jodi Arias: Dirty Little Secret*
April 13, 2015	Sentenced to life in prison without the possibility of parole
2023	Jodi is housed at the Arizona State Prison Complex - Perryville
January 21, 2023	Portrayed by Celina Sinden in Lifetime movie *Bad Behind Bars: Jodi Arias*

Jodi Arias was born on July 9, 1980 in Salinas, California. She became famous for murdering her ex-boyfriend Travis Alexander on June 4, 2008. She inflicted 27 knife wounds, slit his throat and shot him. She was jealous because he was going Cancun with another woman. The evidence was overwhelming against her, including photos left at the scene in a digital camera that showed Arias and Alexander at the scene.

She was convicted of first-degree murder and sentenced to life in prison without the possibility of parole.

Velma Barfield

> "I know that everybody has gone through a lot of pain, all the families connected, and I am sorry, and I want to thank everybody who have been supporting me all these six years."

Date	Events
October 29, 1932	Born Margie Velma Bullard in South Carolina
1949	Marries Thomas Burke; they will have two children
April 4, 1969	Velma leaves home with the two children; upon return, they find the house burned, and Thomas Burke dead
1970	Marries Jennings Barfield, who dies a year later from heart complications
1975	Velma is convicted of seven counts of writing bad checks and sentenced to six months in prison
1976	Velma begins caring for the elderly, working for Montgomery and Dollie Edwards in Lumberton, North Carolina
January 29, 1977	Montgomery Edwards falls ill and dies
March 1, 1977	Dollie Edwards falls ill and dies
June 4, 1977	The husband of 76-year-old Record Lee falls ill and dies, soon after Velma begins acting as her caretaker
February 3, 1978	Velma's boyfriend, Rowland Stuart Taylor, falls ill and dies; an autopsy finds arsenic in his system
May 13, 1978	Velma is caught and charged with the murder of Rowland Stuart Taylor; she is incarcerated at Central Prison in Raleigh, North Carolina in a makeshift death row
November 2,	Dies from lethal injection in Central Prison, Raleigh,

Date	Events
1984	North Carolina

She was born Margie Velma Bullard on October 29, 1932 in South Carolina. She eventually killed at least 6 people, both family as well as people she was a caretaker for. She confessed to four of the killings and was sentenced to death.

On May 13, 1978, Velma was caught and charged with the murder of Rowland Stuart Taylor. She was incarcerated at Central Prison in Raleigh, North Carolina in a makeshift death row.

On November 2, 1984, she died from lethal injection in Central Prison, Raleigh, North Carolina.

Arizona "Ma" Barker

> "...the most vicious, dangerous and resourceful criminal brain of the last decade" (J. Edgar Hoover on Ma Barker)

Date	Events
October 8, 1873	Born Arizona Donnie Clark in Ash Grove, Missouri
1931	Barker-Karpis gang formed, with Alvin "Creepy" Karpis and Fred Barker
November 8, 1931	Barker-Karpis gang kill an Arkansas police chief named Manley Jackson
December 19, 1931	Fred Barker and Creepy Karpis kill Sheriff C. Roy Kelly in West Plains, Missouri
April 26, 1932	Barker-Karpis gang kill A.W. Dunlap in Minnesota
June 17, 1932	Barker-Karpis gang rob a Fort Scott, Kansas bank

Date	Events
July 26, 1932	Barker-Karpis gang rob a Cloud County bank in Concordia, Kansas
September 10, 1932	Brother Arthur joins the Barker-Karpis gang
December 16, 1932	Barker-Karpis gang rob the Third Northwestern National Bank in Minneapolis, killing two policemen
April 4, 1933	Barker-Karpis gang rob a bank in Fairbury, Nebraska
June 1933	Barker-Karpis gang kidnap William Hamm of the Hamm's Brewery family; he is released on June 19, 1933 after a ransom was paid. Frank Nitti may have received part of the ransom payment since the kidnapping occurred on his "turf".
August 30, 1933	August 30, 1933—Barker-Karpis gang rob the Stockyards National Bank of South St. Paul, Minnesota; a police officer is killed
September 22, 1933	Barker-Karpis gang robs two bank messengers and kill a Chicago policeman
January 17, 1934	Barker-Karpis gang kidnap Edward George Bremer, Jr., who is released three weeks later after a $200,000 ransom is paid
January 8, 1935	Arthur Barker arrested in Chicago; the police find a map to Ma Barker's house in Florida
January 16, 1935	Police surround the Florida house; Ma Barker is killed with a Tommy Gun in her hand. Her son Fred is also killed.
October 1, 1935	Relatives claim the bodies of Ma and her son, Fred Barker, and bury them at Williams Timberhill Cemetery in Welch, Oklahoma

Date	Events
1940	Portrayed by Blanche Yurka in the film *Queen of the Mob*
1957	Portrayed by Jean Harvey in docudrama *Guns Don't Argue*
1960	Portrayed by Lurene Tuttle in the film *Ma Barker's Killer Brood*
1961	Portrayed by Joan Blondell in an episode of the TV series *The Witness*
1970	Portrayed by Shelley Winters in *Bloody Mama*
1974	Portrayed by Eileen Heckart in the film *The FBI Story: the FBI Versus Alvin Karpis, Public Enemy Number One*
1996	Portrayed by Theresa Russell in the film *Public Enemies*

Born in Ash Grove, Missouri on October 8, 1873, Ma Barker is most famous for being the titular head of the Barker-Karpis gang, which was made up of her sons Fred Barker, Arthur Barker, and Alvin "Creepy" Karpis. This was one of the most vicious gangs of the tommy-gun era. The gang was known for bank robberies, kidnappings, and murder (especially of law enforcement officials). Their reign of terror ran from 1931/1935.

On January 8, 1935, Arthur Barker was arrested in Chicago. In his possession, the police found a map to Ma Barker's house in Ocklawaha, Florida. On January 16, 1935, the police surrounded the Florida house, and opened fire. Both Fred Barker and his mother were killed. Some accounts said that Ma Barker was killed with a Tommy Gun in her hand.

There is some controversy as to what Ma Barker role was in the Barker-Karpis gang. Most movies about the subject depict Ma Barker as the criminal mastermind behind the gang, ordering her sons and other members of the gang (Creepy Karpis) on criminal "jobs". Karpis later negated the idea that Ma Barker was the head of the gang. Another view is that she acted as a sort of "beard" to the gang – she would find places for the gang to live, acting as the sweet, elderly mother of her various boys. In this story, she didn't actually participate in the crimes, although in today's terms, she certainly could be arrested as an accessory to the gang's crimes, and as an accessory after the fact.

""Ma" and Fred Barker died in the upper left bedroom of this cottage."[25]

So where did the idea she was the head of the gang come from? None other than J. Edgar Hoover, who once said of Ma Barker "[she was]...the most vicious, dangerous and resourceful criminal brain of the last decade". This is possibly to justify the

---

[25] Photo by the The Goodspeeds. Public Domain.

killing of an "old lady" by the FBI, but maybe Ma Barker was more than a "beard" for the gang after all.

Below is a 1935 newspaper article about Ma and the gang.
By WILLIAM VOIGT, Jr.

TULSA, Okla., Mareh 12— Kate "Ma" Barker, who died at the business end of a machine gun as the reputed "brains" of her brood, spent her early years apologizing to the law for her crime-stained young.

When Arthur "Doc" Barker, one cf the four sons born to her, goes to trial in St. Paul, Minn., charged, with kidnaping Edward G. Bremer, Commercial State Bank president, "Ma" Barker will not be there to plead for him as she did when He was a youngster.

When Lloyd, the only other son living, is released from federal prison, "Ma" will not be around to welcome him into the gang which for several years has been on the federal blacklist of "predatory criminal bands". And all because "Ma," at some time in her life, decided to trade pleas and apologies for a "chopper." Perhaps discouraged by the persistence of her boys, "Ma" Barker Joined them.

"Ma" Fell Too

When Freddie Barker, the one with the sharp, rat-like features, fell in that rainstorm of lead that poured through the windows and doors and siding of a house in Oklawaha, Fla., recently, "Ma" Barker fell at his side. The 100-shot drum of the machine gun which she clutched in death, was more than half empty.

She died at the hands of the law she had wheedled and cajoled for more than 20 years, then openly defied. In that period she had schooled herself in the black art of harboring criminals and held a key position in a broad underworld communications network.

After making the final transition she presented the strange picture of a grandmother flitting about the countryside with an outlawed weapon in her hands, a skirted menace to society.

Married At 20

Born Arizona Clark in the little Ozark mining town of Aurora,

Mo., she married George Barker of Aurora when she was 20. In 1900 the family moved to Tulsa, then a hell-roaring young town that had begun to feel the magic touch of oil.

Barker, himself, was a steady worker. For 14 years he was employed as custodian of a building here.

He lives now in Joplin, a worn and lonely little old man, caretaker of a tourist camp. On his sick bed, recently, he was informed of the death of his former wife and one of his sons.

"There's nothing for me to say,", he said weakly. "I don't know anything. All I want is to be kept out of it. A long time ago I decided to go it alone."

And go it alone, he did, leaving "Ma" to entangle her life inextricably with the lives of her outlaw sons, Fred, Lloyd, Arthur and Her man, who was the first of the family to die as result of outlawry.

Not Always "Wanted"

The sons were not always high in the government's "public enemy" list. Once upon a time they were boys playing in old Central Park, in Tulsa, with their crowd.

The "crowd," however, developed into a gang, and in a short time burglaries and thievery and small robberies were marked against them.

"Ma" Barker became a familiar figure at police headquarters, where she seemed always to be pleading the fines and sentences be suspended. Her eternal song was: "My boys would be all right if the law would let them alone."

When the boys grew up they grew deeper in the mire of outlawry. Herman, a bank robber and killer, wanted for a Cheyenne, Wyo., slaying, killed himself rather than be arrested when he was pursued and blinded by an officer's bullet, near Wichita, Kan.

"Doc" Arrested

It was an interstate rubbery affair that sent Lloyd to Leavenworth prison in Kansas. Wanted for the Bremer kidnaping and for violating a parole in Oklahoma where he was serving a life sentence for murder. "Doc" was arrested by department of justice agents in Chicago and sent to St. Paul for federal court trial.

Freddie was wanted In connection as well as for questioning on the cold blooded murder of a West Plains, Mo., sheriff.

Through the nineteen-twenties, Ma" lived in a little shack north of the railroad tracks in Tulsa, trying to "front" for her boys with the law. She took them in when they came there to "cool off" after robberies and other jobs, and the shack became a key point for making contact with other members of the gang and its interlocking membership with other mobs.

Of the old "Central Park mob" of 22, Detective Lieutenant Earl Gardner recalls that nearly half "have been slain by officers and most of the rest are in prison awaiting trial.

Ma Takes To Trail

Ma" made spurious bond once or twice to free her sons so they could "jump" ball and disappear. But officers were unable to prove anything against her. With the criminals who visited her flitting out of town before officers could arrive—due to that communications system of the underworld—it was impossible to obtain necessary evidence.

Soon she began traveling in and out of Tulsa. Shortly before the Bremer kidnapping, she took the road definitely with Freddie and "Doc" and the others of the gang.

"Ma" made her last stand against the officers in a house in Oklawaha, Fla., near a stream of the same name, an Indian name that means "muddy waters."

Not less black and roiled than the waters of the stream were the currents and crosscurrents of her own life, ended as a fugitive, desperately fighting the law she and her flesh and blood had outraged through the years.[26]

---

[26] *The Daily Alaska empire*, March 12, 1935

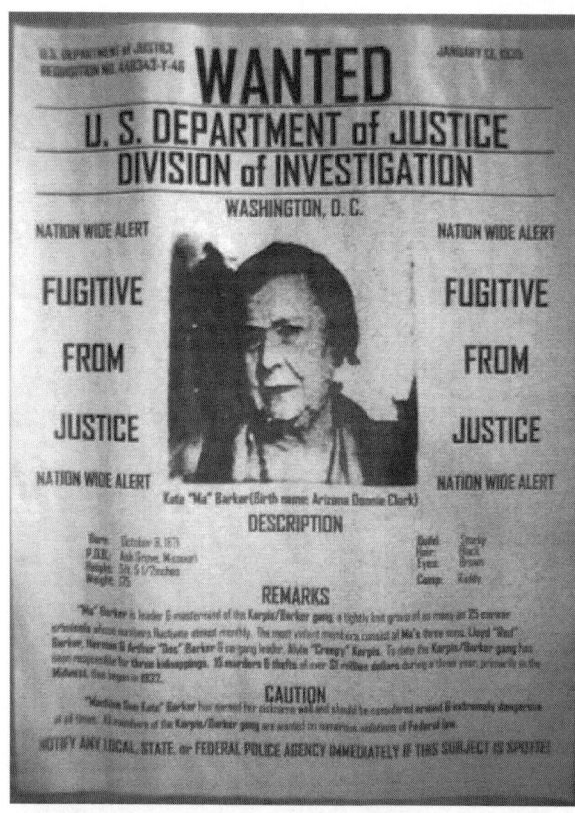

Photo: 1934 Wanted Poster[27]

Juana Barraza

Date	Events
December 27, 1957	Born in Epazoyucan, Hidalgo, Mexico
	Professional wrestler of the name *La Dama del Silencio* (The Lady of Silence)
	Begins murdering women over 60, gaining their trust by claiming she was going to help them receive

---

[27] Public Domain.

Date	Events
	welfare payments
2005	Police begin investigation
January 25, 2006	Suspect seen fleeing the house of Ana María de los Reyes Alfaro, 82, who had just been murdered. Barraza is soon linked to 10 murder victims through fingerprints.
March 31, 2008	Found guilty of 16 murders and other charges
2015	Sentenced to 759 years in Prison for 16 murders

She was born on December 27, 1957 in Epazoyucan, Hidalgo, Mexico. In time, she would become known as the "Little Old Lady Killer." Juana Barraza killed over 30 women, all over the age of 70, in the Mexico City area. In time, she is sentenced to 759 years in prison for 16 murders.

Below is a BBC article on the hunt for the killer, written in 2005.

> Mexico police hunt serial killer
>
> Mexico City police are hunting a serial killer thought to be behind the unusual murders of as many as 15 elderly women.
>
> The suspect - nicknamed "Mataviejitas" or the "Little Old Lady Killer" - is thought to be a man dressed in women's clothes or a well-built woman.
>
> The killer is said to have entered the victims' homes by winning their trust - possibly by posing as a health worker - before beating and strangling them.
>
> The Mexican capital has one of the highest crime rates in the world.
>
> Bizarre coincidence?

Witnesses in the case of an 85-year-old widow killed last month said they saw a large woman in a red blouse - who may also have been a man disguised as a woman - leaving the victim's house.

Mexico City chief prosecutor Bernardo Batiz said the killer was "brilliantly clever", acting alone and winning the confidence of old people.

Three of the last four victims of the killer owned a print of an 18th century painting, Boy in Red Waistcoat, by French artist Jean-Baptiste Greuze.

Prosecutors say this bizarre link may be mere coincidence.

A government body has distributed thousands of leaflets warning the elderly over the killings.

Mexican authorities have been criticized by the United Nations for failing to solve cases of violence against women.

The unsolved murders of hundreds of women in the border city of Ciudad Juarez over the last decade have attracted international attention.[28]

Griselda Blanco

Date	Events
February 15, 1943	Born Griselda Blanco Restrepo in Cartagena, Bolívar, Colombia (some sources say Santa Marta)
1954	Said to have kidnapped a young boy for ransom, and then killed him when the parents of the boy didn't pay up
1963	Marries Alberto Bravo
1970s	Traffics cocaine in New York City with Alberto Bravo
April 1975	Indicted on federal drug conspiracy charges, but flees to Columbia before they can arrest her

---

[28] BBC News, October 11, 2005

Date	Events
1976	Smuggles 13 pounds of cocaine into New York of the ship *Gloria*, which the Colombian government had sent to America as part of a bicentennial race in New York Harbor.
1978	Marries for the third time - Dario Sepulveda. They have a son named Michael (after Michael Corleone in the *Godfather*)
1979	Pioneers motorcycle drive-by shootings
July 11, 1979	Her hitmen kill a rival dealer at the Dade County Shopping Mall; they chase terrified employees through the mall
Late 1970s	Returns to the U.S. and settles in Mami, just as the cocaine wars are heating up
1983	Third husband Dario Sepulveda kidnaps young Michael, and flees to Columbia; eventually, hitmen kill Dario, and return Michael to Griselda
1984	• Has drug dealer Marta Saldarriaga Ochoa killed • Flees to California
February 17, 1985	Arrested in California by the Drug Enforcement Administration and charged with conspiring to manufacture, import, and distribute cocaine. She is eventually sentenced to 15 years.
1992	One of her sons from her first marriage, Osvaldo, is shot and killed by one of Pable Escobar's men
1994	Henchman Jorge Ayala testified against her
1998	Pleads guilty to three Florida murders and is sentenced to 20 years in prison
2002	Heart attack in prison
2004	Released and deported to Columbia
Cocaine Cowboys 2	Prominently featured in the documentary *Cocaine Cowboys*

Date	Events
2007	Last time she is seen – at Bogotá Airport
2008	Prominently featured in documentary *Cocaine Cowboys* and *Cocaine Cowboys 2*
September 3, 2012	Murdered in Medellín by a motorcyclist who entered the butcher shop she was in
2018	Portrayed by Catherine Zeta-Jones in the TV movie *Cocaine Godmother*

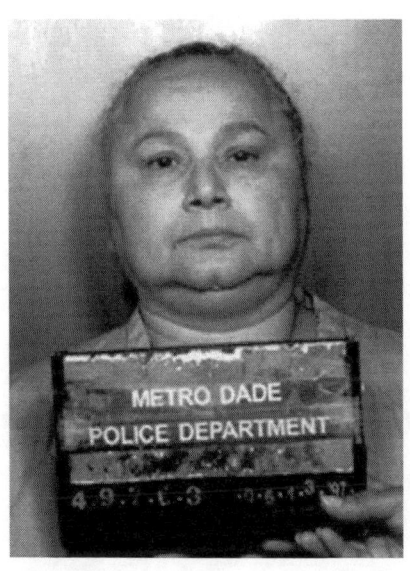

"Mugshot of Griselda Blanco. Colombian drug lord of the Medellín Cartel and a pioneer in the Miami-based cocaine drug trade and underworld during the 1970s and early 1980s."[29]

She was born Griselda Blanco Restrepo in Cartagena, Bolívar, Colombia on February 15, 1943 (some sources say she was born in Santa Marta). She was implicated in 200 murders during her career trafficking cocaine, primarily in the United States.

---

[29] Metro Dade Police Department. Public Domain.

In the early 1970s, she became involved with drug trafficker Alberto Bravo. They moved to New York where they set up a successful cocaine smuggling operation. Griselda was indicted for smuggling cocaine, and she and Alberto fled back to Columbia.

In the late 1970s, Alberto and Griselda returned to the United States, and settled in Miami. In 1979, Griselda pioneered the motorcycle drive-by shooting. On July 11, 1979, she became famous for orchestrating the Dade County Shopping Mall Massacre, where four people were killed.

In 1984, she had drug dealer Marta Saldarriaga Ochoa killed. Griselda then fled to California.

On February 17, 1985, she was arrested in California by the Drug Enforcement Administration and charged with conspiring to manufacture, import, and distribute cocaine. She was eventually sentenced to 15 years.

In 1998, she pled guilty to three Florida murders and was sentenced to 20 years in prison. After having a heart attack in prison, she was released in 2004 and deported to Columbia.

On September 3, 2012, Griselda Blanco was murdered in Medellín by a motorcyclist who entered the butcher shop she was in.

Below is some official information on the 1975 indictment of Griselda Blanco, and her subsequent trial in 1985.

> On April 30, 1975, an indictment charging appellant Griselda Blanco and 37 others was filed in the United States District Court for the Southern District of New York and the case was assigned to Judge John Cannella. The indictment charged the defendants with conspiring to manufacture, import into the United States, and distribute cocaine. By January 1976, twelve of the conspirators had been prosecuted and convicted, and two others had pleaded guilty.

When the indictment was returned in April, 1975, Blanco, a Colombian citizen, was living in Colombia. In May, 1975, the district court issued a warrant for her arrest. That year, Charles Cecil, a special agent of the Drug Enforcement Administration ("DEA"), began investigating Blanco's whereabouts. By 1977, Cecil had learned of her address in Colombia through an informant and he took several measures to keep track of Blanco's whereabouts and to discover whether she entered the United States.

After intensifying its surveillance and investigation of her, the DEA finally arrested Blanco in Irvine, California, on February 17, 1985. Blanco gave a false name to the DEA agents who arrested her and she was found to be carrying false identification papers.

Blanco's jury trial before Judge Cannella commenced on June 25, 1985 and ended July 9, 1985...

The jury returned a verdict of guilty on one count of conspiracy to manufacture, import into the United States, and distribute cocaine. Following Blanco's conviction, the district court held a hearing on Blanco's motion to dismiss the indictment on the grounds that she had been denied a speedy trial. The district court denied this motion on November 6, 1985, finding that the delay was of Blanco's own making. Two days later, the court sentenced Blanco to fifteen years in prison and fined her $25,000...[30]

Leonarda Cianciulli

Date	Events
April 18, 1894	Born in Montella, Avellino, Italy
1917	Marries Raffaele Pansardi
1921	The couple moves to Lauria, Potenza
1927	Leonarda is arrested for fraud, and serves a prison sentence; upon her release, the couple moves to

---

[30] United Nations Office on Drugs and Crime. https://sherloc.unodc.org/cld/case-law-doc/drugcrimetype/usa/1988/united_states_v_blanco.html

Date	Events
	Lacedonia, Avellino
July 23, 1930	Their house is destroyed in the Irpinia earthquake; the couple then moves to Correggio, Reggio Emilia
1939	• Leonarda finds that her son Giuseppe is going to join the Italian army; she decides that sacrifices need to be made to protect her son • Leonarda murders a middle-age woman named Faustina Setti with an axe; Leonarda makes "crunchy" tea cakes out of some of the remains and serves them to lady friends
September 5, 1940	Murders Francesca Soavi with an axe. She makes more tea cakes.
September 30, 1940	Murders Virginia Cacioppo with an axe and boils the remains down into soap. Leonarda later comments that the tea cakes she made from the remains were "very sweet".
1946	Leonarda is tried for murder in Reggio Emilia. She is found guilty of three murders, and sentenced to 30 years in prison, and three years in an asylum.
October 15, 1970	Dies in Pozzuoli, Naples, Italy of cerebral apoplexy
1983	*Love and Magic in Mama's Kitchen* is produced on Broadway

Leonarda Cianciulli was born on April 18, 1894 in Montella, Avellino, Italy. She murdered three women and turned one of the bodies into soap. This earned her the sobriquet of *the soap-maker of Correggio*.

In 1946, Leonarda was tried for murder in Reggio Emilia. She was found guilty of three murders, and sentenced to 30 years in prison, and three years in an asylum. She died on October 15, 1970, in Pozzuoli, Naples, Italy of cerebral apoplexy.

Below is a detailed description of her crimes.

Born in Montella di Avellino in 1893 and marked by an unhappy childhood, in 1914 Leonarda Cianciulli married Raffaele Pansardi, a clerk in the registry office, and went to live in Lariano in Alta Irpinia. In 1930 an earthquake destroyed their home, and the couple moved to Correggio, in the province of Reggio Emilia. Leonarda had seventeen pregnancies: three were miscarriages, while ten of the children died at a tender age. The four surviving children were to be protected at any price, for Leonarda had not forgotten the words of a gypsy fortune-teller who many years earlier had predicted a terrible fate for her: "You will marry and have children, but all your children will die." Later she had had her palm read by another gypsy, who told her: "In your right hand I see prison, in your left a criminal asylum." In 1939, when she heard that her eldest and favourite son Giuseppe was to join the army, as Italy's entry into the war became increasingly imminent, Leonarda decided what she had to do: she had to make human sacrifices to save her son's life. She had three friends, lonely middle-aged women who would give anything to escape from the routine and solitude of Correggio. All three asked Leonarda for help, and she decided that the time had come to act.

The first to fall into her trap was Faustina Setti, the oldest, drawn by Leonarda's promise that she had found her a husband in Pola. Leonarda convinced the woman not to tell anyone about the news. On the day of her departure, Faustina went to say goodbye to her friend, who convinced her to write some letters and postcards to her friends and relatives, which she was to send as soon as she reached Pola, telling them that everything was fine. But Faustina Setti never reached Pola: she was killed with an axe by Leonarda Cianciulli, who dragged the body into a closet and cut it into nine parts, gathering the blood in a basin. Then, as she wrote in her statement, "I threw the pieces into a pot, added seven kilos of caustic soda, which I had bought to make soap, and stirred the whole mixture until the pieces dissolved in a thick, dark mush that I poured into several buckets and emptied in a nearby septic tank. As for the blood in the basin, I waited until it had coagulated, dried it in the oven, ground it and mixed it with flour, sugar, chocolate, milk and eggs, as well as a bit of margarine, kneading all the ingredients together. I made lots of crunchy tea cakes and served them to the ladies who came to visit, though Giuseppe and I also ate them."

The second victim was Francesca Soavi. Leonarda had promised her a job at the girls' school in Piacenza. On the morning of 5 September 1940, she went to say goodbye to her friend before setting off.

The script was the same: Leonarda convinced the woman to write two postcards, telling her she should send them from Correggio to inform her acquaintances that she was leaving, but without saying where she was going. Leonarda then attacked the woman and made the second "sacrifice". The third and final victim was Virginia Cacioppo, a former opera singer, then 53, reduced to living with her memories of the past, in poverty. Leonarda offered her a job in Florence as the secretary to a mysterious theatre impresario, begging her not to tell a soul. Virginia was enthusiastic about the proposal, and kept the secret. On 30 September 1940 she went to Leonarda's house, where: "She ended up in the pot, like the other two (...); her flesh was fat and white, when it had melted I added a bottle of cologne, and after a long time on the boil I was able to make some most acceptable creamy soap. I gave bars to neighbours and acquaintances. The cakes, too, were better: that woman was really sweet."

Virginia's sister-in-law, whose suspicions were aroused by her sudden disappearance, and who had last seen her going into Leonarda Cianciulli's house reported the facts to the Police Superintendent in Reggio Emilia who, by following the many clues left by the murderess, unmasked "the soap-maker". Under questioning Leonarda Cianciulli immediately confessed to the three murders.

The court found her guilty of the atrocious crimes, and sentenced her to thirty years in prison and three years in a criminal asylum. She died in the women's criminal asylum in Pozzuoli on 15 October 1970, struck down by cerebral apoplexy.[31]

---

[31] http://www.museocriminologico.it/correggio_uk.htm

Nannie Doss

Date	Events
November 4, 1905	Born in Blue Mountain, Alabama
1920s/1954	Kills four husbands, two children, her sister, her mother, two grandsons, and a mother-in-law
1921	• Goes to work at Linen Thread Company in Anniston, AL • Marries Charley Braggs, who she had only known 4 months; they would have 4 daughters
1927	• Two daughters die of food poisoning • Braggs flees with the oldest daughter, Melvina
Summer 1928	Braggs returns Melvina; Nannie and Charley divorce
1929	Marries Robert Franklin Harrelson
1943	Melvina gives birth to Robert Lee Haynes
July 7, 1945	Robert dies of asphyxia while in Nannie's care
1945	Nannie kills her husband with rat poison, supposedly after he raped her
1950	Marries Arlie Lanning, who dies, probably of rat poisoning
1950	Moves in with her sister, who dies shortly after
1952	Marries Richard L. Morton
January 1953	Murders her mother
May 19, 1953	Richard L. Morton dies
June 1953	Marries Nazarene minister Samuel Doss
October 12, 1954	Samuel Doss dies of arsenic poisoning
October 1954	Confesses to 8 murders
May 17, 1955	Pleads guilty to the death of Samuel Doss and is sentenced to life imprisonment
1957	A judge declares her insane

Date	Events
June 2, 1965	Dies of leukemia in Oklahoma State Penitentiary, Oklahoma State Penitentiary, McAlester, Oklahoma. She is buried at Oak Hill Memorial Park, McAlester, OK.

Nannie Doss was born on November 4, 1905 in Blue Mountain, Alabama. She would go on to murder almost a dozen people, including various husbands.

Mrs. Nannie Doss[32]

---

[32] *Evening star.* (Washington, D.C.) November 29, 1954

Below is a 1954 newspaper article which discusses the case.

Grandmother Tells of Slaying 4 Husbands With Rat Poison
Oklahoma Woman Describes in Detail How She Took Lives
By the Associated Press

TULSA, Okla., Nov. 29—Mrs. Nannie Doss, an affable grandmother, signed additional statements last night that she used liquid rat poisoning to snuff out the lives of four of her five husbands.

She calmly smoked a cigarette as she described in detail how she put the poison into the food and drink of husbands from four States.

County Attorney J. Howard Edmonston said a murder charge will be filed today against the 49 - year -old, plumpish, jovial widow for the October 6 death of Samuel Doss, 58, of Tulsa.

Police said Mr. Doss was her fifth husband and the second she had met through a "Lonely Hearts" club. It was Mrs. Doss herself who permitted the autopsy starting the investigation that led to her confession.

Four Other Husbands.

Mr. Edmonston said the other poisoned husbands and the dates they died are:
Frank Harrelson, Jacksonville, Ala., 1945.
Harley Lanning, Lexington, N.C., 1952.
Richard L. Morton, 64, Emporia, Kan., May, 1953.

The prosecutor, with city officers and Kansas and Oklahoma agents, has questioned the woman since her arrest Friday night and said investigations into the deaths of four of Mrs. Doss' relatives probably will be undertaken.

He identified the relatives, whom he said died under strange circumstances, as Mrs. Doss' mother, two sisters and a step grandson. After making her confessions Mr. Edmondson related. Mrs. Doss declared, "My conscience is clear." He said it was a comment she uttered after each formal statement.

The only surviving husband of Mrs. Doss is Charley Braggs of Alabama City, Ala. Mr. Edmondson said Mrs. Doss told him the marriage to Mr. Braggs in 1921 produced four daughters, two now living. They were divorced in 1928.

Gives Reasons for Acts.

County Investigator W. A. Land said Mrs. Doss gave the following reasons for poisoning her husbands:

She poisoned Mr. Lanning by doping his food. She said she poisoned him on a Tuesday or a Wednesday and that he died the following Friday.

She declared she had been jealous of Mr. Lanning because he was popular with the women. That was the same reason she gave for placing the rodent killer in the coffee of Mr. Morton, a native of Okmulgee, Okla., and of Indian descent.

She claimed Mr. Harrelson beat her, so she poured liquid poison into his jug of corn whisky. Mr. Edmondson said she denied any connection with the deaths of her sisters, her mother or Mr. Harrelson's 21/2-year-old grandson who preceded Mr. Harrelson in death by two months.

Mrs. Doss permitted an interruption of her interrogation yesterday long enough to make an appearance for television cameramen. She sat through a filmed interview at which only questions from authorities were permitted.

Officers said that before the filming, Mrs. Doss, womanlike, insisted on prettying herself for the occasion. She smiled and seemed to enjoy herself during the brief questioning.

Ernest Harrelson, brother of husband No. 2, claimed Mrs. Doss married his brother in 1945 and that he died the same year. The bespectacled Mrs. Doss asserted she married him in 1929, a year after she divorced Mr. Braggs.

Mrs. Doss told officers she knew Mr. Braggs as a child in Blue Mountain, Ala., and that she married him when she was 15.

Her dead sisters were identified by police as Mrs. Sula Barttee of Gadsen, Ala., who died in 1952, and Mrs. Dovie Weaver of Anniston, Ala., who died in 1951. Officers said Mrs. Doss recalled she nursed both before their death.

She was quoted as saying she poisoned Mr. Morton because "I lost my head and blew up when I found out he had been running around with another woman and had bought some rings."

Mr. Edmondson said she told him she poisoned Mr. Doss twice because "he was mean to me," once by pouring "a lot of poison on his prunes." After eating them he went to the hospital for 23 days. The day after he returned, Mrs. Doss was quoted, she gave him a tablespoonful of poison in a cup of coffee.

Mr. Doss drank the coffee and died the next day at the hospital, she recalled. "He sure did like prunes," she was quoted. "I fixed a whole box and he ate them all."[33]

Belle Gunness

Date	Events
November 11, 1859	Born Bella Paulsdatter or Brynhild Paulsdatter Størset in Selbu, Sør-Trøndelag, Norway
1874	Confirmed at the Evangelical Lutheran Church
1881	Emigrates from Norway to the United States
1884	Marries a rich shopkeeper, Mads Sorenson
July 30, 1900	Her husband dies of a cerebral hemorrhage, and Belle collects $5,000 in insurance money
April 1, 1902	Marries Peter Gunness; a week later, his infant daughter dies mysteriously. Peter dies 8 months later from a skull injury. Belle collected $3,000 in insurance money.

---

[33] *Evening star.* (Washington, D.C.) November 29, 1954

Date	Events
1905	Begins placing marriage ads in Chicago newspapers. Henry Gurholt answers an ad and is never seen again, although his coat and trunk end up in Belle's possession.
1906	John Moe answers an ad, and is never heard from again, although his truck is seen at Belle's house
April 28, 1908	Belle's farm burns to the ground, and numerous bodies are found buried around the farm, many of them disemboweled. A headless body is found that is thought to be Belle's.
November 1908	Ray Lamphere, a farm hand, is arrested for burning down the farm. He testifies that he was asked to do it by Belle Guiness. He says that the headless body that was found is not Belle's. A later, second confession by Lamphere says that he burned the farm down with Belle and her children in it.
2004	Elizabeth Hurley plays an actress portraying Belle Guinness in movie *Method*
2008	DNA tests on the headless body are inconclusive
2021	Traci Lords portrays Belle in *The Farm*

She was born Bella Paulsdatter or Brynhild Paulsdatter Størset in Selbu, Sør-Trøndelag, Norway on November 11, 1859. In 1881, she emigrated from Norway to the United States. She killed over forty husbands, children and rich suitors for insurance money.

In 1884, she married a rich shopkeeper, Mads Sorenson. On July 30, 1900, her husband mysteriously died of a cerebral hemorrhage, and Belle collected $5,000 in insurance money.

On April 1, 1902, Belle married Peter Gunness. A week later, his infant daughter died mysteriously. Peter died 8 months later from a skull injury. Belle collected $3,000 in insurance money.

In 1905, Belle began placing marriage ads in Chicago newspapers. Henry Gurholt answered an ad and was never seen again, although his coat and trunk end up in Belle's possession.

In 1906, John Moe answered an ad, and was never heard from again, although his truck was seen at Belle's house.

On April 28, 1908, Belle's Indiana farm burned to the ground, and numerous bodies were found buried around the farm, many of them disemboweled. A headless body was found that was thought to be Belle's.

On November 1908, Ray Lamphere, a farm hand, was arrested for burning down the farm. He testified that he was asked to do it by Belle Guiness. He says that the headless body that was found is not Belle's. A later, second confession by Lamphere says that he burned the farm down with Belle and her children in it. Thus, it is inconclusive as to whether Belle survived the fire or not.

Belle Gunness[34]

---

[34] Library of Congress https://lccn.loc.gov/2002706295

Mrs. Belle Guiness, of Laporte's Murder Farm[35]

Gwendolyn Graham & Catherine May Wood

Date	Events
March 7, 1962	Born Catherine Wood in Soap Lake, Washington
August 6, 1963	Born Gwendolyn Gail Graham in California
1986	Gwendolyn and Catherine become lovers after meeting at Alpine Manor nursing home in Walker, Michigan
January 1987	The pair murder a woman who had Alzheimer's disease at Alpine Manor nursing home

---

[35] *The Argus*, May 13, 1908

Date	Events
Early 1987	The pair murder four more patients, most with Alzheimer's
1988	Wood's husband goes to the police
December 4/5, 1988	Graham and Wood are arrested and charged with two murders
November 3, 1989	Graham found guilty of five murders and one count of conspiracy to commit murder; she is sentenced to five life sentences. She is incarcerated in the Women's Huron Valley Correctional Facility in Pittsfield Charter Township
	Wood is charged with one count of second-degree murder and one count of conspiracy to commit second-degree murder; she is sentenced to 20 years on each count, and is incarcerated at the minimum security Federal Correctional Institution, Tallahassee in Florida
January 16, 2020	Wood is released
1992	*Forever and Five Days* written by Lowell Cauffiel

Gwendolyn Gail Graham was born in California on August 6, 1963. Catherine Wood was born in Soap Lake, Washington on March 7, 1962. This lesbian couple would become famous for smothering five elderly patients to death.

The two became lovers after meeting at Alpine Manor nursing home in Walker, Michigan in 1986. Looking to spice up their sex life (they had tried asphyxia), the pair murdered a woman who had Alzheimer's disease at Alpine Manor nursing home in January 1987. In early 1987, the pair would murder four more patients, most with Alzheimer's (since they didn't seem to fight back).

In 1988, Wood's husband went to the police, and on

December 4/5, 1988, Graham and Wood were arrested and charged with two murders.

On November 3, 1989, Graham was found guilty of five murders and one count of conspiracy to commit murder - she was sentenced to five life sentences. She was incarcerated in the Women's Huron Valley Correctional Facility in Pittsfield Charter Township.

Wood was charged with one count of second-degree murder and one count of conspiracy to commit second-degree murder and sentenced to 20 years on each count. She was incarcerated at the minimum security Federal Correctional Institution, Tallahassee in Florida. She was released on January 16, 2020.

Wood's lower sentence was as a result of a plea deal whereby she testified against Graham.

"Catherine May Wood & Gwendolyn Graham, 25-year old and 24-year old lesbian couple from Grand Rapids, Michigan who achieved sexual thrills in killing 5 elderly female patients at the nursing home."[36]

---

[36] Kent County Sheriff's Department

Karla Homolka

Date	Events
May 4, 1970	Born Karla Leanne Homolka in Mississauga, Ontario
1987	17-year-old Karla Homolka meets Paul Bernardo at a hotel restaurant
December 23, 1990	Karla and Paul Bernardo rape and murder Karla's sister Tammy
1991	Karla and Paul marry
August, 1991	Karla and her husband Paul Bernardo drug and rape a 15-year-old girl
June 15, 1991	Karla and her husband Paul Bernardo kidnap, rape, torture and murder a 14-year-old girl named Leslie Mahaffy. They dismember her, and dump her in nearby Lake Gibson, encased in concrete.
June 29, 1991	One of the concrete blocks is found by a fisherman
April 16, 1992	Karla and her husband Paul Bernardo kidnap, rape, torture and murder a 15-year-old girl named Kristen French
April 30, 1992	French's nude body is found in a ditch
May 18, 1993	Karla is arraigned on two counts of manslaughter after agreeing to testify against her husband
June 28, 1993	Karla is tried in a secret trial, and gets a 12-year plea deal for helping the prosecution with their case against her husband
February 1994	Karla divorces Paul Bernardo
1995	Karla testifies against Paul Bernardo, who is found guilty of murder and other charges, and sentenced to life imprisonment
2001	Transferred to the Ste-Anne-des-Plaines Institution
2005	• Released from prison after serving her sentence (July 4, 2005) • Senator Michel Biron calls the restrictions

Date	Events
	placed on Karla after her release totalitarian
2006	Portrayed by Laura Prepon in the movie *Karla*
2012	Karla has had three children with her husband Thierry Bordelais (brother of her lawyer)
2017	A Global News article states that Homolka changed her name to Leanne Teale and that she volunteered in a children's school
2021	*Ken and Barbie Killers: The Lost Murder Tapes* airs

Karla Leanne Homolka was born on May 4, 1970 in Mississauga, Ontario. In1987, 17-year-old Karla Homolka met her future husband and partner in crime Paul Bernardo at a hotel restaurant.

Between 1990/92, Karla and Paul raped four young girls, and killed three of them. The first occurred on December 23, 1990, when they raped and murdered Karla's sister Tammy.

On May 18, 1993, Karla was arraigned on two counts of manslaughter after agreeing to testify against her husband. She claimed that he forced her into the raping and killings. On June 28, 1993, Karla was tried in a secret trial, and received a 12-year plea deal for helping the prosecution with their case against her husband.

In 1995, Karla testified against Paul Bernardo, who was found guilty of murder and other charges, and sentenced to life imprisonment. Karla positioned herself as a victim wo was forced to do what her husband wanted. Later, videotapes of their crime spree showed up, and it made clear that she was "all in" on the crimes, just like her husband.

In 2001, she was transferred to the Ste-Anne-des-Plaines Institution. On July 4, 2005, she was released from prison after serving her sentence. Judge Jean R. Beaulieu ruled in a hearing that Karla should have certain restrictions on her, Including:

- She was to tell police her home address, work address and with whom she lives
- She was required to notify police as soon as any of the above changed
- She was likewise required to notify police of any change to her name
- If she planned to be away from her home for more than 48 hours, she had to give 72 hours' notice
- She could not contact Paul Bernardo, the families of Leslie Mahaffy and Kristen French or that of the woman known as Jane Doe (see above), or any violent criminals
- She was forbidden to be with people under the age of 16
- She was forbidden from consuming drugs other than prescription medicine
- She was required to continue therapy and counselling
- She was required to provide police with a DNA sample

Genene Jones

Date	Events
July 13, 1950	Born in Texas
1968	Marries high school sweetheart; they will have two children
Late 1970s	Nursing school
1970s/1980s	Murdered up to 60 infants as a licensed vocational nurse at Bexar County Hospital and at a facility in Kerryville, Texas
1984	Convicted of murder of one child
1985	Sentenced to 99 years in prison for killing 15-

Date	Events
	month-old Chelsea McClellan with succinylcholine
1991	Portrayed by Susan Ruttan in TV movie *Deadly Medicine*
2002	Portrayed by Alicia Bartya in movie *Mass Murder*
May 2016	Serving time at the Lane Murray Unit of the Texas Department of Criminal Justice
May 25, 2017	Indicted for the murder of 11-month-old Joshua Sawyer. This was to prevent her mandatory release as part of a prison overcrowding program.
April 2018	A judge refuses to throw out new murder charges against Genene
January 16, 2020	Pleads guilty to the murder of 11-month-old Joshua Sawyer; sentenced to life in prison

Genene Jones was born on July 13, 1950, in Texas. She was found guilty of murdering 2 infants, but it is possible that she killed up to 46 children.

She would inject infants in her care with digoxin, heparin and later succinylcholine. The infants would become very sick, and Genene would swoop in and "save" them. Sometimes, they died anyway, as happened to 14-month-old Chelsea McClellan who was brought to the hospital for a regular immunization for mumps and measles. She died of a heart attack, and investigations ensued. In 1985, she was sentenced to 99 years in prison for killing 14-month-old Chelsea McClellan with succinylcholine.

On May 25, 2017, she was indicted for the murder of 11-month-old Joshua Sawyer. This was to prevent her mandatory release as part of a prison overcrowding program. On January 16, 2020, she pled guilty to the murder of 11-month-old Joshua Sawyer and was sentenced to life in prison.

"Drawing shows lawyer speaking in front of others during the trial of Genene Jones for the murder of a child"[37]

---

[37] Library of Congress https://lccn.loc.gov/2019632749

Manson Girls

"Drawing shows three women talking amongst themselves, possibly Susan Atkins, Patricia Krenwinkel, and Leslie Van Houten, while seated behind Charles Manson during a trial for the Sharon Tate and the LaBianca murders"[38]

Three women went to trial along with Charles Manson for the murders of Sharon Tate *et al* and Mr. and Mrs. LaBianca. At the time the three caused quite a sensation, as they sang together on their way to the court room, wore miniskirts, and were all attractive. All were convicted and sentenced to death, but later their sentences were lessened to life in prison.

All three protested Manson's innocence.

---

[38] Library of Congress. https://lccn.loc.gov/2016652853

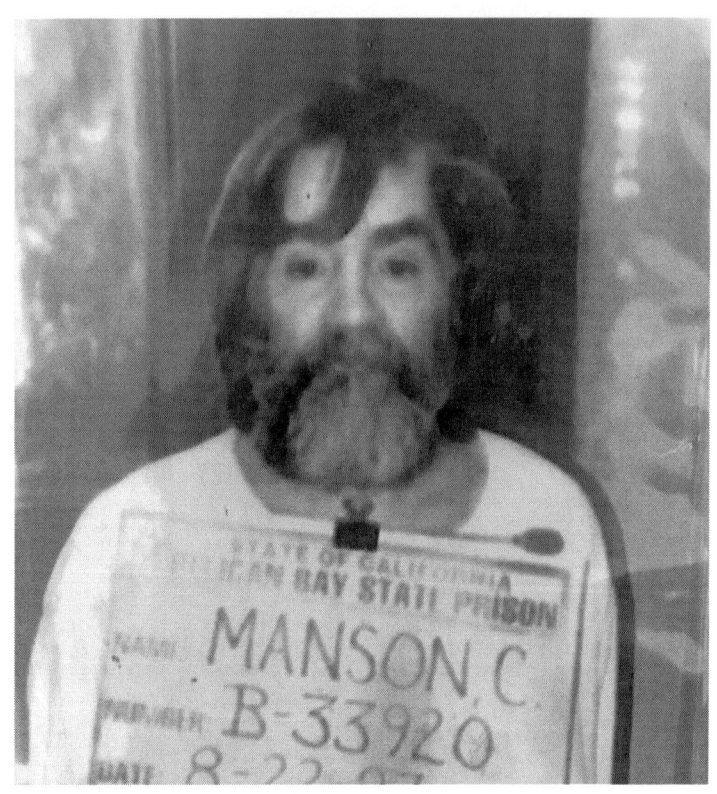

Charles Manson in a 1997 prison mugshot[39]

The question often arises about the motive of the three women involved in the Tate/LaBianca murders. I can't speak for any of them, but Charles Manson kept them drugged on LSD the whole time they lived at Spahn Ranch.

---

[39] California Department of Corrections and Rehabilitation. Public Domain.

Barker Ranch, Death Valley, home of the Manson family during parts of 1969 (Photo by Robert C. Jones)

Susan Atkins

Date	Events
May 7, 1948	Born Susan Denise Atkins in San Gabriel, California
1967	Meets Charles Manson at the San Francisco house she was staying in
October 7, 1968	Bears a son by Bruce White, at Spahn Ranch
July 25, 1969	Manson sends Atkins, Bobby Beausoleil, and Mary Brunner to the home of Gary Hinman, to try to coerce money from him (the rumor was that he had inherited money). Beausoleil beat him up when Hinman tried to explain that he had no inheritance. Manson later showed up and attacked Hinman with a sword.
July 27, 1969	Beausoleil kills Hinman after Hinman signs over the registration of his two cars.
August 7, 1969	Beausoleil is arrested for the murder of Gary

Date	Events
	Hinman
August 8, 1969	Manson sends Atkins, Linda Kasabian, and Patricia Krenwinkel along with Tex Watson to murder the inhabitants of the home of Roman Polanski. Susan Atkins writes "Pig" on the front door with the blood of Sharon Tate.
August 9, 1969	Atkins, Krenwinkel, Watson, Linda Kasabian, Leslie Van Houten, and Steve "Clem" Grogan accompany Manson to the home of Leno and Rosemary LaBianca in order to murder them. Manson leaves before the killing begins.
October 1969	Several different law enforcement agencies, including National Park Service Rangers, officers from the California Highway Patrol and the Inyo County Sheriff's Offices raid Barker Ranch, and arrest most of the gang. Susan Atkins is charged with the murder of Gary Hinman and ends up in prison.
	Later, Atkins blabs to prison associates that she was involved in the Tate/LaBianca murders. She is arrested for her part in the murders, along with Van Houten, Krenwinkel, Kasabian, and Watson.
	Atkins appears before a grand jury and testifies about the events surrounding the Tate/LaBianca killings. She states that she stabbed Frykowski in the legs and told Sharon Tate that she had no sympathy for her.
June 15, 1970	Murder trial for Manson, Atkins, Krenwinkel and Van Houten begins
March 29, 1971	Atkins is sentenced to death
April 23, 1971	Atkins is transferred to California's new death row prison for women. In 1972, her death sentence was

Date	Events
	commuted to life imprisonment, when the death penalty was judged illegal by the state supreme court (People v. Anderson).
1974	Becomes a born-again Christian
1976	Portrayed by Nancy Wolfe in the 1976 made-for-TV film *Helter Skelter*
September 2, 1981	Marries Donald Lee Laisure; they divorce in 1982
1987	Marries James W. Whitehouse, who was serving as her lawyer at the time
2000	Sharon Tate's sister Debra appears at the Parole hearing of Susan Atkins
2003	Files a Federal lawsuit claiming she was a political prisoner
June 1, 2005	At her 17th parole hearing, she is granted a three-year denial
2003	Portrayed by Maureen Allisse in *The Manson Family*
2004	Portrayed by Marguerite Moreau in remake of *Helter Skelter*
June 1, 2005	Requests compassionate leave from prison because of an undisclosed illness
April 2008	Atkins has her left leg amputated
July 15, 2008	Compassionate release hearing held; her request is turned down
September 24, 2008	Transferred back to the Central California Women's Facility in Chowchilla, California
2009	Portrayed by Anjelica Scannura in *Manson, My Name Is Evil*
September 2, 2009	Susan is denied parole for the final time
September 24, 2009	Dies in Chowchilla, California

Date	Events
2014	Portrayed by Devanny Pinn in *House of Manson*
2015	Portrayed by Ambyr Childers in the TV series *Aquarius*
2019	Portrayed by Mikey Madison in *Once Upon a Time in Hollywood*.

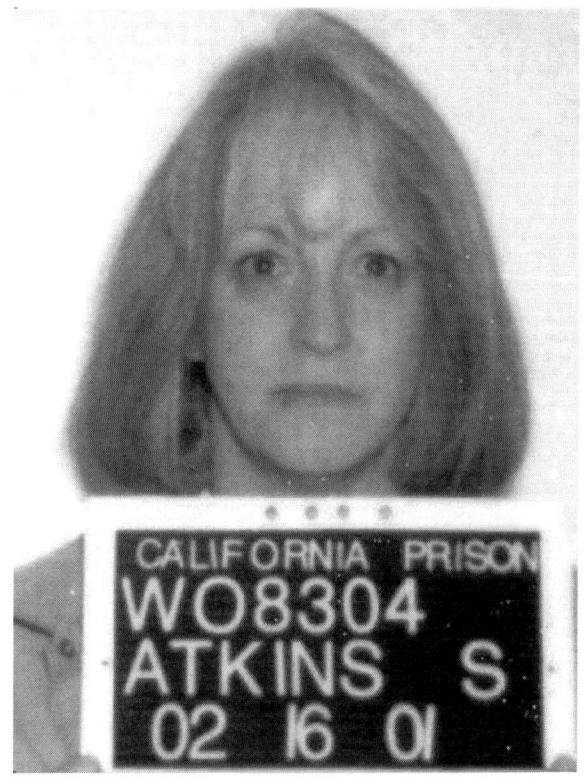

"Mugshot taken of Susan Atkins, taken 16 February 2001"[40]

Other than Squeaky Fromme, who tried to assassinate the President, Susan Atkins is probably the best known of the Manson girls. She was born Susan Denise Atkins in San

---

[40] California Department of Corrections. Public Domain.

Gabriel, California on May 7, 1948. She would eventually be charged with 8 murders, having been part of both the Tate/LaBianca murders, as well as the Gary Hinman murder.

She met Charles Manson in 1967 in San Francisco. On October 7, 1968, she bore a son by Bruce White, at Spahn Ranch.

On July 25, 1969, Manson sent Atkins, Bobby Beausoleil, and Mary Brunner to the home of Gary Hinman, to try to coerce money from him (the rumor was that he had inherited money). Beausoleil beat him up when Hinman tried to explain that he had no inheritance. Manson later showed up and attacked Hinman with a sword. On July 27, 1969, Beausoleil killed Hinman after Hinman signed over the registration of his two cars.

On August 8, 1969, Manson sent Atkins, Linda Kasabian, and Patricia Krenwinkel along with Tex Watson to murder the inhabitants of the home of Roman Polanski. Susan Atkins is the one who wrote "Pig" on the front door with the blood of Sharon Tate.

The next evening, August 9, 1969, Atkins, Krenwinkel, Watson, Linda Kasabian, Leslie Van Houten, and Steve "Clem" Grogan accompanied Manson to the home of Leno and Rosemary LaBianca in order to murder them. Manson left before the killing began.

The murders were "successful" in that the authorities had no idea who had perpetrated them, and in fact didn't link them at first. In October 1969, several different law enforcement agencies, including National Park Service Rangers, officers from the California Highway Patrol and the Inyo County Sheriff's Offices raided the Barker Ranch in Death Valley, and arrested most of the gang. Susan Atkins was charged with the murder of Gary Hinman and ended up in prison.

Later, Atkins blabbed to prison associates that she was involved in the Tate/LaBianca murders. She was arrested for her part in the murders, along with Van Houten, Krenwinkel, Kasabian, and Watson.

She appeared before a grand jury and testified about the events surrounding the Tate/LaBianca killings. She stated that she stabbed Frykowski in the legs and told Sharon Tate that she had no sympathy for her.

On June 15, 1970, the murder trial for Manson, Atkins, Krenwinkel and Van Houten began. On March 29, 1971, Atkins was sentenced to death. On April 23, 1971, Atkins was transferred to California's new death row prison for women.

In 1972, her death sentence was commuted to life imprisonment, when the death penalty was judged illegal by the state supreme court (People v. Anderson).

On June 1, 2005, Atkins requested compassionate leave from the prison because of an undisclosed illness (probably terminal brain cancer). Her request was eventually denied. In April 2008, after having been hospitalized for a month, Atkins had her left leg amputated.

On July 15, 2008, a compassionate release hearing was held – her request was turned down.

On September 24, 2008, Atkins was transferred back to the Central California Women's Facility in Chowchilla, California. On September 2, 2009, she was denied parole for the final time. Between 1976 and 2009, she was denied parole a total of 13 times. She died on September 24, 2009, in the Chowchilla, California facility.

At the time of her death, she was the longest incarcerated female prisoner in the California penal system. After her death, she was overtaken by the other two Manson girls.

Lynette ""Squeaky" Fromme

Date	Events
October 22, 1948	Born Lynette Alice Fromme in Santa Monica, California
1966	Graduates from Redondo Union High School
1967	Becomes second member of Manson's family
1968	Elderly Ranch owner George Spahn gives her the nickname "Squeaky"
August - October 1969	The family, including Squeaky, migrates to the Barker House in Death Valley
October 1969	Several different law enforcement agencies, including National Park Service Rangers, officers from the California Highway Patrol and the Inyo County Sheriff's Office raid Barker Ranch, and arrest most of the gang. Squeaky, Krenwinkel and Manson are among those arrested for the theft of a road grader in Death Valley.
June 15, 1970	Protests Manson's innocence at the Tate/LaBianca trial; she refuses to testify, and serves a brief prison sentence
November 1972	Brought in for questioning for a series of murders in Sacramento, but is eventually released for lack of evidence
1973	Starts working on a 600-page book on the Manson Family named *Reflexion*

Date	Events
September 5, 1975	Attempts to assassinate President Gerald Ford with a Colt M1911 .45-caliber semi-automatic pistol; the gun had 4 bullets in the magazine, but none in the chamber. She eventually receives a sentence of life imprisonment.
1979	Attacks a fellow inmate with a hammer
December 23, 1987	In an attempt to meet Charles Manson, she escapes from Federal Prison Camp Alderson in West Virginia
July 2008	Granted parole on her original sentence, but had to serve extra time because of her prison escape
August 14, 2009	Released on parole, and moves to New York
2018	*Reflexion: Lynette Fromme's Story of Her Life with Charles Manson 1967–1969* is finally published
2019	- Professes that she is still in love with Charles Manson - Portrayed by Dakota Fanning in Quentin Tarantino's film *Once Upon a Time in Hollywood*

She was born Lynette Alice Fromme on October 22, 1948 in Santa Monica, California. While not part of the Tate/LaBianca murders, she would go on to fame for trying to assassinate President Gerald Ford.

In 1967, she became the second member of Manson's Family. She was with him at the house of Dennis Wilson, the Spahn Ranch and the Barker House in Death Valley. She was one of the Family members arrested at the Barker Ranch in October 1969.

Starting on June 15, 1970, she participated in protests outside of the Tate/LaBianca trial. She loudly proclaimed Manson's innocence. She refused to testify and served a brief prison sentence for contempt of court.

Lynette "Squeaky" Fromme, second from left[41]

On September 5, 1975, she attempted to assassinate President Gerald Ford with a Colt M1911 .45-caliber semi-automatic pistol. The gun had 4 bullets in the magazine, but none in the chamber. The police later found the ejected cartridge on the floor in her apartment. She eventually received a sentence of life imprisonment.

In July 2008, she was granted parole from her original sentence, but had to serve extra time because of an earlier prison escape. She was finally released on parole on August 14, 2009. She moved to New York and continued to profess her love for Charles Manson.

Below is a statement by her on her Website.

> "I went to the Capitol and came to court specifically to draw attention to the problems of the world that directly affect my state of mind and my physical body and to offer a way to clean up the world. This is my intent."

---

[41] http://airtreeswateranimals.blogspot.com/p/rainbow.html

"In this mind is the face of Charlie, but MANSON is the Mind. The Shaman, the seer, the visionary. He wears all crowns from thorns to precious gems and metals to cloth and beads, feathers, bone, sinew, fiber, and the dangling windwisps of whispered spirit and breath. He is the mind of all, of much unseen, unimagined or unrealized, of all we don't understand and all we fear..."

"How can the social system be improved? It's a crime to smoke marijuana, a plant, but poisoning millions of people through toxic wastes is business as usual. How much will you give up for the lives of your children's children, which is yourself. How much are people willing to give up for Air, Earth. Water, Animals, and the coming generations? I think the answer to that is pretty clear."

"Almost everything you eat or drink has water in it. No matter where it's from, most of it's polluted. Most of it's got a lot of chemicals that we have to stop producing, it's a simple thing. We don't transfer it. We don't move the poisons somewhere else. We stop producing them. We use our brains."

"I do not have the answers and as a woman I do not intend to play my own thoughts over the truth. I can clearly state the problems and tell you that I suffer from them."[42]

Leslie Van Houten

Date	Events
August 23, 1949	Born Leslie Louise Van Houten in Altadena, California
1966	Homecoming Princess at Monrovia High School in Monrovia, California
Summer 1968	Moves in with Catherine Share and Bobby Beausoleil
1968	Catherine Share and Leslie move into the commune of Charles Manson at Spahn Ranch; heavy LSD use follows
August 9, 1969	Patricia Krenwinkel, Leslie Van Houten, and Tex

---

[42] https://atwaatwar.blog/2011/10/22/red/

Date	Events
	Watson murder Rosemary and Leno LaBianca on orders from Manson
August 16, 1969	Police raid Spahn Ranch looking for stolen autos, but don't find any. Manson and his followers leave Spahn Ranch soon after, and head to the Barker Ranch in Death Valley.
October 1969	Several different law enforcement agencies, including National Park Service Rangers, officers from the California Highway Patrol and the Inyo County Sheriff's Office raided Barker Ranch, and arrest most of the gang
June 15, 1970	Murder trial for Manson, Atkins, Krenwinkel and Van Houten begins
March 29, 1971	Leslie is convicted of murder, and sentenced to be executed
Early 1970s	Leslie works with a social worker named Karlene Faith, who attempts to separate her from her identification with Manson
February 18, 1972	California Supreme Court overturns the death penalty, and commutes Leslie's sentence to life in prison
1975	Moved to general population at the California Institution for Women (the Manson women had been housed separately until then)
1976	Portrayed by Cathey Paine in made-for-TV film *Helter Skelter*
1977	Retrial results in a hung jury
Second retrial	Guilty, with life imprisonment, but eligible for parole
2003	Portrayed by Amy Yates in *The Manson Family*
2004	Portrayed by Catherine Wadkins in *Helter Skelter*
2009	Portrayed by Kristen Hager in *Leslie, My Name Is Evil*

Date	Events
2013	Her request for parole is turned down for the 20th time
2015	Portrayed by Emma Dumont in NBC TV show *Aquarius*
2016	- Portrayed by Tania Raymonde in the film *Manson Girls* - Portrayed by Greer Grammar in *Manson's Lost Girls*
April 14, 2016	A two-person panel of the California Parole Board recommended granting Van Houten's parole application, but it is rejected by Governor Jerry Brown
September 29, 2016	Los Angeles County Superior Court Judge William C. Ryan issues an 18-page ruling backing Brown's rejection of the parole application
December 21, 2016	California Supreme Court denies Van Houten's petition to hear the case
September 6, 2017	21st parole hearing; her request is approved by the two-person panel, but then rejected by Governor Jerry Brown
2018	- Portrayed by Gabrielle Klobucar in *Inside the Manson Cult: The Lost Tapes* - Portrayed by Hannah Murray in the movie *Charlie Says*
2019	Portrayed by Victoria Pedretti (as Lulu) in *Once Upon a Time in Hollywood*
January 30, 2019	At her 22nd parole hearing, parole is approved, but rejected by Governor Gavin Newsom
September 21, 2019	An appeals court panel rules 2–1 against reversing Newsome's rejection
July 23, 2020	Her parole application is approved, but then rejected by Governor Gavin Newsom

Date	Events
November 9, 2021	Her parole application is approved, but then rejected by Governor Gavin Newsom
February 9, 2022	California Supreme Court rejects her request for a review

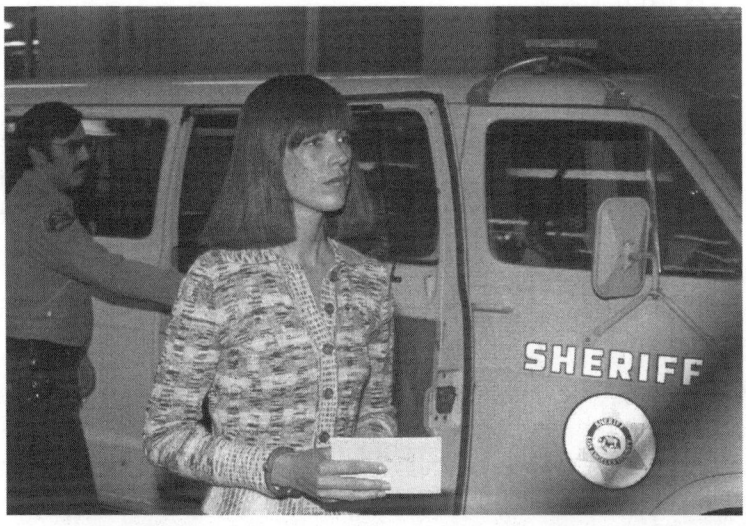

"Leslie Van Houten arrives at the Criminal Courts Building in Los Angeles for a rearraignment and hearing on setting a new trial date for her role in the LaBianca murders"[43]

She was born Leslie Louise Van Houten in Altadena, California on August 23, 1949. In time, she would be convicted and sentenced to death for the murder of Leno and Rosemary LaBianca on August 9, 1969.

She first came in contact with the Manson family in the Summer of 1968 when she moved in with Catherine Share and

---

[43]*Los Angeles Times*, December 27, 1976, Creative Commons Attribution 4.0 International license.

Bobby Beausoleil. Catherine Share and Leslie then moved into the commune of Charles Manson at Spahn Ranch. Heavy LSD use followed.

On August 9, 1969, Patricia Krenwinkel, Leslie Van Houten, and Tex Watson murdered Rosemary and Leno LaBianca on orders from Manson.

A week later, police raided Spahn Ranch looking for stolen autos, but didn't find any. Manson and his followers would leave Spahn Ranch soon after, and head to the Barker Ranch in Death Valley.

In October 1969, several different law enforcement agencies, including the National Park Service Rangers, officers from the California Highway Patrol and the Inyo County Sheriff's Office raided the Barker Ranch, and arrested most of the gang. Ironically, Manson and his followers were not apprehended for the Tate/LaBianca/Hinman murders, but rather for the arson of a Death Valley "Michigan Articulating Loader" near the Lippincott Mine a month before (as well as various auto theft, stolen property and firearms charges).

On June 15, 1970, the murder trial for Manson, Atkins, Krenwinkel and Van Houten began. Atkins, Krenwinkle and Van Houten would become famous for locking arms and singing on their way to the courtroom.

On March 29, 1971, Leslie was convicted of murder, and sentenced to be executed. On February 18, 1972, the California Supreme Court overturned the death penalty, and commuted Leslie's sentence to life in prison

In 1977, her retrial resulted in a hung jury. The second retrial returned a guilty, with life imprisonment, sentence but with one major change – she was eligible for parole.

Her eligibility for parole has not really helped her. Beginning in 2016, the parole board has recommended parole for her several times, but they were quickly overridden by the governor each (Jerry Brown once, Gavin Newsome, twice.)

Patricia Dianne Krenwinkel

Date	Events
December 3, 1947	Born Patricia Dianne Krenwinkel in Los Angeles, California
1965	Graduates from Westchester High School
September 12, 1967	Joins Manson family
June 21, 1968	Arrested for drug possession
Summer 1968	Along with Ella Bailey, picked up by Dennis Wilson (Beach Boys) while cruising around Los Angeles
August 1968	Krenwinkel and others persuade George Spahn to allow the Manson family to stay on the Spahn Ranch
August 8, 1969	Participates in the murders at 10050 Cielo Drive, home of actress Sharon Tate and her husband, director Roman Polanski; she stabs Abigail Folger multiple times
August 9, 1969	Participates in the murder of Leno and Rosemary LaBianca with help from Tex Watson, Clem Grogan and Leslie Van Houten
August 16, 1969	Krenwinkel, Manson and others are arrested at Spahn Ranch for auto theft, but are soon released because of a date error on the search warrant
August - October 1969	The family, including Krenwinkel, migrates to the Barker House in Death Valley
October 1969	Several different law enforcement agencies, including National Park Service Rangers, officers from the California Highway Patrol and the Inyo

Date	Events
	County Sheriff's Office raid Barker Ranch, and arrest most of the gang. Krenwinkel, Manson, and Squeaky Fromme are among those arrested for the theft of a road grader in Death Valley
December 1, 1969	Arrested near her aunt's house in Mobile, Alabama
December 2, 1969	Indicted for seven counts of first-degree murder (Sharon Tate Polanski, Abigail Ann Folger, Wojciech Frykowski, Steven Earl Parent, Jay Sebring, Leno and Rosemary La Bianca) and one count of conspiracy to commit murder
February 1970	Krenwinkel waives extradition hearings and voluntarily returns to California
June 15, 1970	Manson, Krenwinkel, Van Houten, and Atkins go on trial (Watson is extradited to Texas).
March 29, 1971	Guilty on all counts and sentenced to death. Transferred to California Institution for Women (CIW) near Corona, California.
1972	Her death sentence is commuted to life imprisonment, when the death penalty is judged illegal by the state supreme court (People v. Anderson)
1976	Portrayed by Christina Hart in the made-for-TV film *Helter Skelter*
July 17, 1978	First parole hearing
2003	Portrayed by Leslie Orr in the film *The Manson Family*
2004	Portrayed by Allison Smith in the remake of *Helter Skelter*
January 2011	Parole turned down; she would not be eligible for another hearing for seven years
2013	• Portrayed by Kaniehtiio Horn in *Leslie, My*

Date	Events
	Name Is Evil • Portrayed by Vanessa Zima in *Manson Girls*
2015	Portrayed by Madisen Beaty in the TV series *Aquarius*
June 22, 2017	Denied parole (her 14th time)
2018	Portrayed by Sosie Bacon in *Charlie Says*
2019	Portrayed by Madisen Beaty in *Once Upon a Time in Hollywood*
May 26, 2022	Granted Parole; overridden by Governor Gavin Newsome

Patricia Krenwinkle, 1973[44]

She was born on December 3, 1947 as Patricia Dianne Krenwinkel in Los Angeles, California. She joined the Manson family in September 1967.

In the Summer of 1968, she was picked up by Dennis Wilson

---

[44] Creative Commons Attribution 4.0 International license, by Reppop.

(Beach Boys) while cruising around Los Angeles. The Manson family would spend several weeks squatting at his house.

In August 1968, Krenwinkel and others persuaded elderly George Spahn to allow the Manson family to stay on the Spahn Ranch. They would remain there until October 1969.

On August 8, 1969, she participated in the murders at 10050 Cielo Drive, home of actress Sharon Tate and her husband, director Roman Polanski. Patricia stabbed Abigail Folger multiple times.

The next night, August 10, 1969, Patricia participated in the murder of Leno and Rosemary LaBianca with help from Tex Watson, Susan Atkins, Clem Grogan and Leslie Van Houten.

On August 16, 1969, Krenwinkel, Manson and others were arrested at Spahn Ranch for auto theft but were soon released because of a date error on the search warrant. As a result of increased notice from the police, the family, including Krenwinkel, migrated to the Barker Ranch in Death Valley.

In October 1969, several different law enforcement agencies, including National Park Service Rangers, officers from the California Highway Patrol and the Inyo County Sheriff's Office raided Barker Ranch, and arrest most of the gang. Krenwinkel, Manson, and Squeaky Fromme were among those arrested for the theft of a road grader in Death Valley.

On December 1, 1969, Krenwinkle was arrested near her aunt's house in Mobile, Alabama. On the next day, she was indicted for seven counts of first-degree murder (Sharon Tate Polanski, Abigail Ann Folger, Wojciech Frykowski, Steven Earl Parent, Jay Sebring, Leno and Rosemary La Bianca) and one count of conspiracy to commit murder. In February 1970, Krenwinkel waived extradition hearings and voluntarily returned to California.

The trial started on June 15, 1970. Manson, Krenwinkel, Van Houten, and Atkins went to trial (Watson was extradited to Texas).

On March 29, 1971, Patricia Krenwinkle was found guilty on all counts and sentenced to death. She was transferred to the California Institution for Women (CIW) near Corona, California.
In 1972, her death sentence was commuted to life imprisonment, when the death penalty was judged illegal by the state supreme court (People v. Anderson). She was now eligible for parole.

On May 26, 2022, she was granted parole (her 15th try), but it was overridden by Governor Gavin Newsome. She remains incarcerated.

Nazis

Some of the evilest women in history worked for the SS in several concentration camps in Germany, including Ravensbruck, Buchenwald, Auschwitz, Bergen-Belsen and others. They were given ranks in the camps, but weren't really considered part of the SS. The ranks included:

- Chef Oberaufseherin, "Chief Senior Overseer" [Ravensbrück]
- Lagerführerin, "Camp Leader"
- Oberaufseherin, "Senior Overseer"
- Erstaufseherin, "First Guard" [Senior Overseer in some satellite camps]
- Rapportführerin, "Report Leader"
- Arbeitsdienstführerin, "Work Recording Leader"
- Arbeitseinsatzführerin, "Work Input Overseers"
- Blockführerin, "Block Leader"
- Kommandoführerin, "Work Squad Leader" [Senior Overseer in some satellite camps]
- Hundeführerin, "Dog Guide Overseer"
- Aufseherin, "Overseer"
- Arrestführerin, "Arrested Overseer"[45]

There were about 3,600 female concentration camp guards during the war (some sources say 5,000). 78 of them were tried after the war.

---

[45] https://en.wikipedia.org/wiki/Female_guards_in_Nazi_concentration_camps

Dorothea Binz

Date	Events
March 16, 1920	Born in Försterei Dusterlake, Province of Brandenburg, Weimar Republic
August 1939	Volunteers for kitchen work at Ravensbruck
September 1940	Deputy director of her penal block
Summer 1942	Director of the cell block
February 1944	Promoted to *Stellvertretende Oberaufseherin* (Deputy Chief Wardress)
May 3, 1945	Captured by the British in Hamburg
1947	Prosecuted for War Crimes at the Ravensbrück trial
April 1947	Sentenced to death
May 2, 1947	Hung at Hamelin Prison, Hamelin, Allied-occupied Germany

Dorothea Binz was born on March 16, 1920 in Försterei Dusterlake, Province of Brandenburg, Weimar Republic. She rose to the rank of *Stellvertretende Oberaufseherin* (Deputy Chief Wardress) of Ravensbruck in February 1944.

On May 3, 1945, she was captured by the British in Hamburg, and prosecuted for War Crimes at the first Ravensbrück trial in 1947. She was sentenced to death, and hung at Hamelin Prison, Hamelin, Allied-occupied Germany in April 1947.

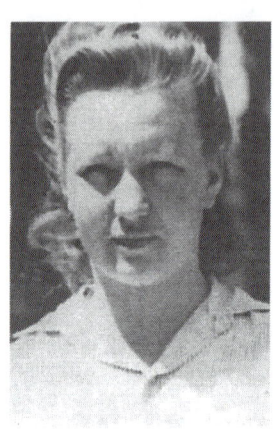

Dorothea Binz[46]

Therese Rosi Brandl

Date	Events
February 1, 1902	Born in Staudach-Egerndach, Bavaria, German Empire
1940	*SS Aufseherin* in KZ Ravensbrück
1942	Transferred to Auschwitz; eventually becomes *Erstaufseherin* (First Guard)
Summer 1943	Receives the war service medal for her work in concentration camps
November 1944	Transferred to Muehldorf (a satellite camp of Dachau); Made selections for the gas chambers
April 27, 1945	As the American army nears, Therese flees Muehldorf
August 29, 1945	Arrested in the Bavarian mountains by the U.S. Army
November 1947	Tried by Polish authorities
December 22,	Convicted of selecting inmates for termination

---

[46] Public Domain.

Date	Events
1947	
January 24th, 1948	Hung at Montelupich Prison in Krakow, Poland

Therese Rosi Brandl was born on February 1, 1902 in Staudach-Egerndach, Bavaria, German Empire. During the war years, she served at several concentration and extermination camps, including Ravensbrück, Auschwitz and Muehldorf. In 1943, she received the war service medal for her work in concentration camps.

On August 29, 1945, she was arrested in the Bavarian mountains by the U.S. Army. In November 1947, she was tried by Polish authorities, and, on December 22, 1947 she was convicted of selecting inmates for termination. She was hung at Montelupich Prison in Krakow, Poland on January 24th, 1948.

Irmgard Furchner

Date	Events
1925	Born in Germany
June 1943 / April 1945	Works as a secretary/stenographer in Stutthof concentration camp; 60,000 people are murdered there
End of World War II	Marries SS squad leader Heinz Furchtsam (d. 1972)
September 2021	Hours before her trial was to begin, Irmgard apparently fled when she took a cab to the Norderstedt Mitte subway station; an arrest warrant was issued, and she was soon caught
2022	Charged with 11,412 counts of accessory to murder and 18 additional counts of accessory to attempted murder. Found guilty.

Date	Events
December 20, 2022	Given two year suspended sentence

In late 2022, people around the world were fascinated that a 96-year-old woman who lived in a nursing home was charged with 11,412 counts of accessory to murder. Of course, Irmgard Furchner wasn't some crazed serial killer. Rather, this was probably that last woman who will ever be charged for Nazi war crimes.

Her defense was that she was just a secretary, and that she didn't know anything about any deaths in the Stutthof concentration camp. However, it was noted in court that 1) she worked in commandant Paul-Werner Hoppe's office and 2) the position of her desk allowed an excellent view of the area where prisoners were brought into the camp. An historian who testified at the trial noted that 27 transports carrying 48,000 people arrived at Stutthof between June and October 1944.

She didn't help her case when, at the end of the War, she married SS squad leader Heinz Furchtsam (d. 1972).

On December 20, 2022, she was found guilty of being an accessory to over 10,000 murders and given a two year suspended sentence. It will be something to talk about in the recreation room at the nursing home.

Crematoria of Stutthof, photographed after liberation, 1945[47]

Irma Grese

> I was born on 7 October 1923. In 1938 I left the elementary school and worked for six months on agricultural jobs at a farm, after which I worked in a shop in Lychen for six months. When I was 15 I went to a hospital in Hohenlychen, where I stayed for two years. I tried to become a nurse but the Labor Exchange would not allow that and sent me to work in a dairy in Fürstenberg. In July 1942, I tried again to become a nurse, but the Labour Exchange sent me to Ravensbrück Concentration Camp, although I protested against it. I stayed there until March 1943, when I went to Birkenau Camp in Auschwitz. I remained in Auschwitz until January 1945. (Irma Grese)

Date	Events
October 7, 1923	Born Irma Elisabeth Ilse Ida Grese in Wrechen, Weimar Republic

---

[47] Public Domain.

Date	Events
c. 1937	Her father, Alfred Grese, joins the Nazi Party
1938	Leaves school; works on a farm, in a shop and then two years in a SS hospital
1941	Works at the SS Female Helpers' training base near Ravensbrück
1942	Becomes a prison guard at Ravensbrück Concentration Camp; promoted to *Aufseherin* (guard or overseer)
March 1943	Transferred to Auschwitz
Autumn 1943	Promoted to Senior SS-Supervisor, in charge of 30,000 women prisoners
1944	Promoted to *Rapportführerin* (Informant-Leader)
January 1945	Returns to Ravensbrück Concentration Camp
March 1945	Transferred to Bergen-Belsen, where she acted as warden of the women's section
April 17, 1945	Captured by the British at Bergen-Belsen
September 17/ November 17, 1945	Belsen trial. Irma is sentenced to hang by a British court
December 13, 1945	Hanged at Hamelin Prison, Hamelin, Germany
2003	Portrayed by Nina Young in the made for TV movie *Out of the Ashes*
2005	Portrayed by Sheyla Shehovich in the movie *Pierrepoint*

Irma Grese was born on October 7, 1923 as Irma Elisabeth Ilse Ida Grese in Wrechen, Weimar Republic. During the war, she served as a guard at Ravensbrück, Auschwitz and Bergen-Belsen (warden).

In Autumn 1943, she was promoted to Senior SS-Supervisor at Auschwitz, in charge of 30,000 women prisoners. In 1944, she was promoted to *Rapportführerin* (Informant-Leader). During her time at Auschwitz, she was known as the "Hyena of Auschwitz".

In January 1945, she returned to Ravensbrück Concentration Camp. Two months later, she was transferred to Bergen-Belsen, where she acted as warden of the women's section.

On April 17, 1945, she was captured by the British at Bergen-Belsen. From September 17/November 17, 1945, she was on trial at the Belsen trial. Irma was sentenced to hang by a British court. On December 13, 1945, she was hanged at Hamelin Prison, Hamelin, Germany. She sang Nazi songs the night before her execution.

"Irma Grese standing in the courtyard of the Prisoner of War cage at Celle with Josef Kramer. Both were convicted of war crimes and sentenced to death. 1945"[48]

Below is from the case notes of the Belsen trial. Looking at her responses, she evidently thought that she was as blameless as

---

[48] The Imperial War Museum photograph BU 9745

the day is long.

This accused said that she went to Auschwitz in March, 1943, and remained there until 18th January, 1945. At first she did telephone duties in the Block Leader's room. Then she was put in charge of the Strafkommando (Punishment Party) for two days. After this she worked on another Kommando and later censored mail. Then she became an Overseer in lager C. She only carried a revolver because she was ordered to do so. She never struck anyone so as to cause bleeding or unconsciousness, nor did she kick any prisoners on the ground, or shoot at prisoners. She never took part in selections at Auschwitz, but agreed that selections were made. Szafran's allegations were untrue.(Footnote 1: See p. 13.) Jews were nearly always paraded naked for the gas selection. Her duty at these parades was to keep order, and she admitted that she beat prisoners for running away. She did not know at the time the purpose of the parades. She did not remember the events described She admitted that she beat people in Lager C with a whip made by Stein. (Footnote 2: See p. 14.) of cellophane and with a stick, and that even carrying whips was against Kramer's orders. She gave Overseers under her orders to beat prisoners in order to keep discipline and to prevent stealing in the camp of which she was in charge, but she was not authorised to do this. When prisoners tried to evade parades she thrashed them.

Her answer to Rozenwayg's story (Footnote 3: See pl 16.) was that she had never been with Lothe on an outside working party, and she never had a dog. Ilse Lothe did not work under her as a kapo. Grese denied the truth of the stories told by Watinik, Diament, Kopper, Lobowitz and Trieger, (Footnote 4: See pp. 25,29,35 and 37) and thought that Dunklemann's account (Footnote 5: Seep, 26) of an alleged beating was, if true at all, grossly exaggerated. She denied that she made prisoners hold their hands up above their heads with stones in them. She said that the deponent[49] Catherine Neiger (Footnote 1: See p. 31) was never in her camp.

She came to Belsen in March, 1945. Transports were arriving almost daily, the camp was overcrowded and the prisoners were

---

[49] "a person who makes a deposition or affidavit under oath"

dirty and ill. Roll-calls were held twice a week. She took over the duty of Arbeitsdienstfüherin and went into the woods with working parties, and performed various other duties. She did not beat anyone in Belsen except a kapo who did not work but lay in the sun. She never had any kind of weapon at Belsen, and only struck with her hand. Regarding Sunschein's and Klein's allegation, (Footnote 2: See pp. 17 and 20.) she said that she once saw two parcels which contained meat being thrown away by someone in a group of prisoners. She asked who had done this, and as they would not answer she said that they must make sport until they did. The prisoners made sport for half an hour and then she was told who had thrown the parcels away. She did not report this incident as she thought that the prisoners had been sufficiently punished. Frieda Walter and Irene Haschke, said Grese, worked in No. 3 kitchen at Belsen.[50]

Irmgard Huber

Date	Events
1901	Born in Hadamar (Hessen), Germany
1932	Becomes a nurse
1945	Sentenced to 25 years as an accomplice to murder by an American court
1947	Sentenced to an additional 8 years in prison by a West German court as an accomplice to 120 murders
1952	Although sentenced to 33 years, Irmgard is released
1983	Dies in Hadamar (Hessen), Germany

Irmgard Huber was born in Hadamar, Germany in 1901. In 1932, she became the Chief nurse at Hadamar psychiatric hospital, one of six major euthanasia facilities in Nazi Germany. These facilities were set up to murder people with

---

[50] CASE No. 10., THE BELSEN TRIAL, TRIAL OF JOSEF KRAMER AND 44 OTHERS, BRITISH MILITARY COURT, LUNEBURG, 17TH SEPTEMBER-17TH NOVEMBER, 1945 Part V

mental illness and physical infirmities.

In 1945, she was sentenced to 25 years as an accomplice to murder by an American court. Two years later, she was sentenced to an additional 8 years in prison by a West German court as an accomplice to 120 murders.

Thus, she was sentenced to 33 years in prison, but she was released in 1952.

Interrogated by War Crimes investigators[51]

---

[51]National Archives and Records Administration, Photograph #73720

TEARS FAILED TO HELP —Irmgard Huber, former chief nurse at the Hadamar Insane Asylum, weeps during cross-examination at war criminals trial in Wiesbaden, Germany. She and six other Germans were tried for the murder of 400 Poles and Russians at the asylum. She was sentenced to 25 years' imprisonment.— AP Wirephoto.

Irmgard Huber[52]

Ilsa Koch

Date	Events
September 22, 1906	Born Margarete Ilse Köhler in Dresden, Saxony, German Empire
1921	Accountancy school
1932	Joins the Nazi party
1936	• Guard and secretary at Sachsenhausen concentration camp (her fiancée was

---

[52]*Evening star.* October 06, 1945

Date	Events
	commandant) • Marries Karl-Otto Koch (d. 1945)
1937	The Kochs move to Buchenwald where Ilsa becomes *SS-Aufseherin* (overseer)
1940	Builds an indoor gym, financed mostly by money stolen from inmates (250,000 reichsmarks)
1942	The Kochs are transferred to Majdanek
August 24, 1943	Arrested with her husband on orders by Josias von Waldeck-Pyrmont, SS and Police Leader for Weimar on charges of personal enrichment, embezzlement, and murdering witnesses
1944	Ilsa Koch is acquitted of the SS charges
April 5, 1945	Kurt Otto-Koch is executed after being found guilty by a SS court
June 30, 1945	Arrested by the U.S. Army in Ludwigsburg
1947	Tried by a U.S. military court at Dachau (General Military Government Court for the Trial of War Criminals). The charge: "participating in a criminal plan for aiding, abetting and participating in the murders at Buchenwald".
August 19, 1947	Sentenced to life imprisonment for "violation of the laws and customs of war"
June 8, 1948	Her sentenced is lessened to four years by Gen. Lucius D. Clay, then interim military governor of the American Zone in Germany, because of lack of evidence of the most egregious charges
November 27, 1950	Ilsa is re-tried by a West German court for crimes against German nationals
January 11, 1951	Sentenced to life imprisonment by a German court for "incitement to murder, incitement to attempted murder and incitement to the crime of committing grievous bodily harm"

Date	Events
April 22, 1952	Her appeal is rejected by the Federal Court of Justice
1967	Commits suicide at Aichach Women's Prison in West Germany
1975	Portrayed by Dyanne Thorne in exploitation film *Ilsa, She Wolf of the SS*. Three more films would follow.
2009	Documentary *The Bitch of Buchenwald* released

Ilse Koch, also known as "Ilse of Buchenwald or "The W(B)itch of Buchenwald", was born on September 22, 1906 as Margarete Ilse Köhler in Dresden, Saxony, German Empire. During the war, she served as an overseer at Buchenwald and Majdanek. She is perhaps the most famous of all female Nazi war criminals.

In 1936, she became a guard and secretary at Sachsenhausen concentration camp where her fiancée was commandant. In that year, she married Karl-Otto Koch (d. 1945).

In 1937, the Kochs moved to Buchenwald where Ilsa became SS-*Aufseherin* (overseer). In 1940, she built an indoor sports arena, financed mostly by money stolen from inmates (250,000 reichsmarks).

In 1942, the Kochs were transferred to Majdanek Concentration Camp.

On August 24, 1943, she was arrested with her husband on orders by Josias von Waldeck-Pyrmont, SS and Police Leader for Weimar on charges of personal enrichment, embezzlement, and murdering witnesses. Ilse was eventually acquitted, but Kurt Otto-Koch was executed after being found guilty by a SS court on April 5, 1945.

She was arrested by the U.S. Army in Ludwigsburg on June 30, 1945, and tried in 1947 by a U.S. military court at Dachau (General Military Government Court for the Trial of War Criminals). The charge: "participating in a criminal plan for aiding, abetting and participating in the murders at Buchenwald". She was said to have been involved in murdering prisoners for their tattoos at Buchenwald.

On August 19, 1947, she was sentenced to life imprisonment for "violation of the laws and customs of war". On June 8, 1948, in a controversial move, her sentenced was lessened to four years by Gen. Lucius D. Clay, then interim military governor of the American Zone in Germany, because of lack of evidence of the most egregious charges (including the tattoo situation.)

On November 27, 1950, Ilsa was re-tried by a West German court for crimes against German nationals, and sentenced to life imprisonment for "incitement to murder, incitement to attempted murder and incitement to the crime of committing grievous bodily harm"

In 1967, she committed suicide at Aichach Women's Prison in West Germany.

Her modern fame comes from a series of films made starting in 1975, the first being *Ilsa, She Wolf of the SS.* She was portrayed by a scantily-clad Dyanne Thorne in four films.

Woody Guthrie wrote a song about her.

"Ilse Koch leaves the courtroom with her co-defendants during the trial of former camp personnel and prisoners from Buchenwald."[53]

Ilse Koch testifies in her own defense[54]

---

[53] United States Holocaust Memorial Museum. Public Domain.
[54] United States Holocaust Memorial Museum. Public Domain.

Johanna Langefeld

Date	Events
March 5, 1900	Born in Kupferdreh, Germany
1924	Marries Wilhelm Langefeld (d. 1926)
1935	Works as a guard in a Arbeitsanstalt (working institution) in Brauweiler
1937	Joins Nazi Party
March 1938	Prison guard at Lichtenburg concentration camp
March 1939	Female superintendent of Lichtenburg
May 1939	Moved to Ravensbruck. In charge of *14f13* murder campaign.
March 1942	In charge of building the new women's camp at Auschwitz; made selections for the gas chamber there
July 18, 1942	Heinrich Himmler confirms that the women's camp should be run by a woman
July 1942	After an injury requiring surgery, Johanna is transferred back to Ravensbruck
Ravensbruck	Accused of treating the Polish prisoners too well; the SS arranges to put her on trial
December 20, 1945	Arrested by the United States Army
September 1946	Transferred to Polish authorities for trial
December 23, 1946	Escapes from prison with the help of her former (Polish) prisoners
c. 1957	Lives with sister in Munich
January 26, 1974	Dies in Augsburg, Germany
2019	*The Female Guard – The Case of Johanna Langefeld*

Date	Events
	documentary released

Johanna Langefeld was born on March 5, 1900 in Kupferdreh, Germany. She worked at camps at Lichtenburg (where she rose to the rank of Female superintendent), Ravensbruck (where she was in charge of the *14f13* murder campaign), and Auschwitz (where she was put in charge of building the new women's camp. At Auschwitz, she made selections for the gas chambers.

All of this was sufficient to have her prosecuted for War Crimes and hung, but a strange thing happened on the way to the gallows. In 1942, after being transferred back to Ravensbruck, she was accused at being too lenient to some of the Polish prisoners.

On December 20, 1945, she was arrested by the United States Army, and transferred to Polish authority for trial in September 1946. On December 23, 1946, she escaped from prison with the help of her some of her former Polish prisoners at Ravensbruck.

In 1957, she went to live with her sister in Munich. She died in 1974 in Augsburg.

Johanna Langefeld (Public Domain)

Maria Mandel

Date	Events
January 10, 1912	Born in Münzkirchen, Austria-Hungary
October 15, 1938	Works as a *Aufseherin* at Lichtenburg concentration camp in the Province of Saxony
May 15, 1939	Moves to Ravensbrück concentration camp near Berlin
April 1, 1941	Joins the Nazi Party
April 1942	Promoted to *SS-Oberaufseherin*
October 7, 1942	Assigned to Auschwitz II-Birkenau as *SS-Lagerführerin*, in charge of all women prisoners; involved in prisoner selections for the gas chambers
1943	Creates the *Women's Orchestra of Auschwitz*
	Awarded *War Merit Cross 2nd class*
November 1944	Assigned to Mühldorf subcamp of Dachau concentration camp
August 10, 1945	Arrested by the U.S. Army
November 1946	Transferred to Polish authorities
November 1947	Tried by the *Supreme National Tribunal in the Auschwitz trial*; found guilty of crimes against humanity
January 24, 1948	Hung by Polish authorities at Montelupich Prison in Kraków

If there was a contest for most evil woman criminal, Maria Mandel would be in the running. In her "career", she worked at Ravensbrück, Auschwitz II-Birkenau and Dachau, and she sent an estimated 500,000 women and children to their deaths in the gas chambers at Auschwitz I and II.

Mandel was born on January 10, 1912, in Münzkirchen, Austria-Hungary. After a stint at Ravensbruck, on October 7, 1942 she was assigned to Auschwitz II-Birkenau as *SS-Lagerführerin*, in charge of all women prisoners. As such, she was involved in prisoner selections for the gas chambers.

In 1943, she created the Women's Orchestra of Auschwitz. Around the same time, she was awarded the War Merit Cross 2nd class.

On August 10, 1945, arrested by the U.S. Army and transferred to Polish authorities in November 1946. A year later, she was tried by *the Supreme National Tribunal* in the Auschwitz trial. She was found guilty of crimes against humanity.

On January 24, 1948, she was hung by Polish authorities at Montelupich Prison in Kraków.

Below is the testimony of a former Jewish prisoner at Auschwitz.

> In August 1943 I was deported together with my family (27 people, including nine children aged from one month to eleven years) from the ghetto in Środula near Sosnowiec to Auschwitz, in a transport numbering some 5,000 people.
>
> At the ramp in Birknau, the transport was awaited by the defendant Mandl accompanied by SS woman Margot Drechsel, and as soon as the transport had arrived, Mandl carried out a selection, sending approximately 90 percent of the transport to the cars which transported these people to the nearby crematorium.
>
> [...] During these selections, defendant Mandl tortured the prisoners in a cruel way, beating the women, the men and the children with a whip and kicking them blindly. She would tear the children from the arms of their mothers, and when the mothers tried to come near the children and defend them, Mandl would beat the mothers horribly and kick them. I saw – right next to me – a young, 20-year-old mother, who tried to go near her two-year-old child thrown onto the car, and Mandl kicked and beat her so

cruelly that she didn't get up any more.

[...] I held my four-year-old child by the hand. The defendant Mandl approached me, tore my child away from me and threw the child onto a still empty car so that the child got wounded in the face and began to cry and call me, but I was put aside to the group that wasn't loaded onto the cars. When I tried to reach the child, crying on the car, Mandl began to beat me so cruelly that I fell. Mandl continued to kick me although I was lying on the ground, and she knocked out almost all of my teeth with her shoe.[55]

Photograph of Maria Mandl after her arrest by U.S. Army troops on August 10th, 1945.[56]

Elisabeth Volkenrath

Date	Events
September 5, 1919	Born in Schönau an der Katzbach, Silesia
October 1941	Begins as an unskilled worker at Ravensbrück concentration camp; trained under SS supervisor Dorothea Binz
March 1942	Assigned to Auschwitz Birkenau

---

[55] Jewish Prisoner Sala Feder on December 1, 1947 to the District Court in Kraków
[56] Public Domain.

Date	Events
1943	Marries SS-Rottenführer Heinz Volkenrath
November 1944	Promoted to *Oberaufseherin* (supervising wardress) over all female prisoners at Auschwitz
February 1945	*Oberaufseherin* at Bergen-Belsen
April 1945	Arrested by the British Army
November 1945	Convicted of war crimes at the 1st Belsen trial and sentenced to hang
December 13, 1945	Executed (by hanging) at Hamelin Prison, Hamelin, Allied-occupied Germany

"SS women camp guards are paraded for work in clearing the dead. Elisabeth Volkenrath (second from right, partially hidden) and Herta Bothe (first from right). Elisabeth Volkenrath was head wardress of the camp and sentenced to death. She was hanged on December 13 1945."[57]

Another young woman that married an SS officer and quickly moved up the concentration camp ranks was Elisabeth Volkenrath. She was born on September 5, 1919 in Schönau

---

[57] Imperial War Museums photograph BU 4065

an der Katzbach, Silesia. In her career in the SS, she worked at several camps, including Ravensbrück, Auschwitz Birkenau and Bergen-Belsen. In November 1944 she was promoted to *Oberaufseherin* (supervising wardress) over all female prisoners at Auschwitz. She would later hold the same position at Bergen-Belsen. This position would later get her hung.

In April 1945, she was arrested by the British Army. In November 1945, she was convicted of war crimes at the 1st Belsen trial and sentenced to hang (as was Irma Grese). The sentence was carried out on December 13, 1945 when she was executed (by hanging) at Hamelin Prison, Hamelin, in Allied-occupied Germany.

Below is her statement from the First Bergin Trial. I note with some amusement that her reason for committing the acts she did was under orders from Maria Mandel. Mandel sent something like 500,000 women to die.

"Statement of Elisabeth Volkenrath, SS Oberaufseherin.

I am 26 years of age and come from Schönau near Badlandeck, Silesia. I am a married woman, my husband being in the SS, and I have not heard of him for a long time. Before being called up into the SS I was a hairdresser. In 1939 I was called up to work in a munitions factory and on 1st October, 1942, was transferred to the SS. I never actually became a member of the SS; we merely wore the uniform and became supervisors at concentration camps.

On joining the SS I was sent to Ravensbrück, where I became an Aufseherin and was taught how to treat prisoners. We were told that we were not to talk to prisoners and our job was to take them to work and see that they didn't escape. I later went into the concentration camp at Ravensbrück, where I worked under SS woman Langefeld and Kommandant Koegel. In March, 1942, I was transferred to Auschwitz where I remained until 18th January, 1945. I then proceeded to Bergen-Belsen where I arrived after a long train journey on 5th February 1945.

On arrival at Auschwitz I was placed in charge of a working party sewing clothes. I later was placed in charge of the parcels department where Red Cross parcels from families were received for the prisoners. I always made it my duty to see that the parcels were delivered and those prisoners that worked under me can say that this is true. On 20th September, 1944, I took over a working camp in Auschwitz consisting of a cobbler's shop and tailor's shop which were run for the benefit of the prisoners. I remained at this post until the camp was cleared. Whilst I was at Auschwitz the Kommandanten of the camp were Kommandant Hoess, Liebehenschel and Baer. On the women's side there were SS women Langefeld, Mandel and Drechsel. Kramer was the Kommandant at Birkenau from June or July, 1944, to December, 1944.

I often heard about the gas chamber from prisoners but I never actually saw it although from the distance I have seen the crematorium. I have been present when selections were made from prisoners by the SS Doctors of those unfit to work. These people were all sent to Block 25 and to my knowledge they were never seen again. Oberssturmführer Müller always told us that these people were being sent away to recuperate. Whilst I was at Auschwitz the camp was visited by Himmler and he saw the conditions that existed there.

I have always been very strict, but have never murdered anyone. I have boxed the ears of girls if they did anything wrong but anything I did was always on orders from Lagerführerin Mandel and Drechsel. It was on the orders of Kommandant Kramer that girls were brought to the office and made to make 'sport'. It was conducted by Camp Altesten. This was a punishment for being in possession of things they should not have and consisted of running round the room, bending their knees and generally doing physical exercises. I have always tried as far as possible not to forget that I was a woman and a human being. I was never present when this took place and it only happened once in Block 2.

The many deaths at Belsen were caused by lack of food and overcrowding. Prisoners were marched from other camps to Belsen with little or no food and arrived in an exhausted condition. I mentioned this to Kramer and Vogler. Kramer told me about the 20th March, 1944, that he made a report about the camp and as a result at the end of March, 1945, it was inspected by Pohl, Hoess and Verwirrtungschef Burge and also Dr. Lolling who was head of all doctors in Germany. Due to this inspection temporary barracks should have been built and a start was made in the women's camp at the end of March.

I know things have been bad in these camps but they were also bad for us and we could do nothing about it. We were punished the same as the prisoners by money being stopped, up to 5 marks by Kramer, and confinement to Camp on orders from Berlin, and kept almost the same as the prisoners ourselves. It is true that I have had to make prisoners on Appell hold their hands above their heads but it was always on orders from others; this happened in Auschwitz on instructions from Mandel and Drechsel.

It is my opinion that the man most responsible for the conditions at Auschwitz was Hoess as he was in charge of all camps in this area. Reichsführer Himmler is, of course, responsible for all concentration camps. At no time did I see any orders in writing relating to concentration camps.

On arrival at Belsen I did not work for the first six weeks at all owing to the fact that I was ill. I then took charge of all SS women and received my orders direct from Kommandant Kramer.

Signed Volkenrath, Elisabeth.[58]

---

[58] Transcript of the Official Shorthand Notes of 'The Trial of Josef Kramer and Forty Four Others'

Bonnie Parker

Date	Events
October 1, 1910	Born Bonnie Elizabeth Parker in Rowena, Texas
September 25, 1926	Marries Roy Thornton
January 1929	Bonnie never sees her husband again (dies 1937)
	Meets postal worker Ted Hinton while working as a waitress
January 5, 1930	Bonnie and Clyde meet at the home of Clarence Clay in West Dallas
1932	Ted Hinton joins the Dallas County Sheriff's Department
April 19, 1932	Bonnie is caught with Barrow crony Ralph Falts during a failed hardware store burglary in Kaufman, Texas; Bonnie is released from jail after several months
March 1933	Bonnie and Clyde and Clyde's family members set up housekeeping in Joplin, Missouri
March 23, 1933	Ivan M. "Buck" Barrow, brother of Clyde, is released from prison. Buck and his wife Blanche join the Bonnie and Clyde gang.
April 13, 1933	The police raid the house in Joplin, and Bonnie lays down covering fire with a BAR
May 20, 1933	A warrant is issued for Clyde Barrow and Bonnie Parker, regarding a stolen automobile
November 22, 1933	Bonnie and Clyde narrowly escape a trap set by the Dallas, Texas sheriff
January 16, 1934	Bonnie and Clyde help five prisoners escape from the Eastham State Prison Farm at Waldo, Texas
April 1, 1934	Bonnie and Clyde shoot two patrolmen in Grapevine, Texas

Date	Events
April 6, 1934	Bonnie and Clyde kill a constable in Miami, Oklahoma
May 21, 1934	Bonnie and Clyde have a party in Black Lake, Louisiana, and are said to return to the area in a couple of days
May 23, 1934	Bonnie and Clyde ambushed in Bienville Parish, Louisiana with 130 bullets
1967	Portrayed by Faye Dunaway in the film *Bonnie and Clyde*

Clyde and Bonnie filled with lead before they can use machine guns[59]

Bonnie and Clyde were probably the most famous male/female criminal duo of all time. Together, they murdered nine policemen and four civilians. They went on a crime spree in the 1930s that included robbing banks and stores, kidnappings and, of course, murder.

Bonnie was born on October 1, 1910 as Bonnie Elizabeth Parker in Rowena, Texas. She first met Clyde Barrow on January 5, 1930. It was crime at first site with the two – they would be a duo until the day they died in 1934.

On April 19, 1932, Bonnie was caught with Barrow crony Ralph

---

[59] *Brownsville Herald*, May 24, 1934

Falts during a failed hardware store burglary in Kaufman, Texas. She served several months in jail as a result. Bonnie was released from jail after several months.

In March 1933, Bonnie and Clyde and Clyde's family members set up housekeeping in Joplin, Missouri. Clyde's brother Buck and his sister-in-law joined the gang during this time.

On April 13, 1933, the police raided the house in Joplin, after receiving complaints from the neighbors. Bonnie laid down covering fire with a Browning Automatic Rifle (BAR).

On January 16, 1934, Bonnie and Clyde helped five prisoners escape from the Eastham State Prison Farm at Waldo, Texas. Less than three months later, they shot two patrolmen in Grapevine, Texas.

Five days later, they (April 6, 1934), they killed a constable in Miami, Oklahoma.

On May 23, 1934, Bonnie and Clyde were ambushed in Bienville Parish, Louisiana with 130 bullets in their car. Former Texas Ranger Frank Hamer led the posse that ambushed the two. The coroner J. L. Wade later reported that Barrow sustained seventeen bullet wounds and Parker twenty-six.

Several movies, television series, and songs have been made about the couple, including the film *Bonnie and Clyde* released in 1967 where Bonnie was portrayed by Faye Dunaway. The same year, a hit record named *The Ballad of Bonnie and Clyde* was released by English singer Georgie Fame.

"A snapshot of criminal Bonnie Parker smoking a cigar, seized by police 4-13-1933"[60]

Below are two newspaper accounts (from the same paper) on the ambush that killed Clyde Barrow and Bonnie Parker.

> Barrow Killing Recounted
> Deputy Tells Story pf Climactic Moments of Ten Month Search for Outlaw and Girl.

---

[60] FBI. Public Domain.

A 10 months' search ended lor Bob Alcorn, Dallas County, Tex. deputy sheriff, with the killing of Clyde Barrow and his cigar-smoking. quick-shooting companion, Bonnie Parker. Alcorn, one of the party that ambushed the pair, tells here the story of the slaying.
BY BOB ALCORN.

ARCADIA, La., May 24.—For 10 months I had been trying to get Clyde and Bonnie, 10 months when I did little else except look for them, hope I'd find them and get them dead or alive. Today we got them. They won't kill any one else now.

We got them as they came along the road. It was all over in a moment. Both were dead as their car nosed into a sandbank and came to a stop. They didn't even fire a shot, but they had grabbed at their guns when our bullets knocked them over.

I began following Clyde and Bonnie last Summer. I got reports they
were here, there and yonder, but always, when the other officers and I got there, they were gone. Only once, last November, we ran onto them near Dallas, but they got away when we let them have it and they weren't even hit.

Wide Area Searched.
Since then, I've been after them and, for the last four weeks, I've done nothing else all over East and South Texas. Southern Arkansas, Northern Louisiana and even over into Mississippi, where we heard they had been, but they were always gone when we got there.

A few days ago. we got reports that Clyde and Bonnie had been through this part of the country and had been over the road through Gibbsland. We hung around watching, but nothing happened. We didn't give up. though, and decided to stick around awhile longer.

At 2 o'clock this morning we hid our car in the woods eight miles south of Gibbsland and lay down behind a little knoll. The grass was wet with heavy dew and it was awful, just lying there and waiting. We were right on top of a hill and could see the road until it went over the top of the hill north of us and the other hill south of us.⁶¹

SHERIFF RELATES BARROW KILLING
Account Narrates Six Weeks' Work That Ended Outlaw's Career.
Copyright. 1934. by the Associated Press.

Sheriff Henderson Jordan of Bienville Parish, eyewitness to the slaying of Bonnie Parker and Clyde Barrow, has written the following exclusive account of the killing for the Associated Press.

ARCADIA. La. May 24.— I have been working on this case about six
weeks. I received a "tip" Wednesday that Clyde Barrow and Bonnie Parker were coming through the lower part of Bienville Parish and going to the northern part of Natchitoches Parish.

We began checking. I put an under cover man on this job. I had him stationed in Shreveport. Upon getting a tip that Barrow and Parker figured on robbing the First National Bank of Arcadia. I got in touch with Frank Hamer, ex-captain of Texas Rangers, and R. F. Alcorn, Dallas County deputy sheriff. I had to get someone who knew Barrow and Parker personally in order not to make a mistake in shooting them if we found them.

Tuesday night I received a tip they would be on the Jamestown Sailes road yesterday morning. With Capt. Hemer. Alcorn, Ted Hinton, Dallas deputy, and P. M. Oakley, one of my Bienville Parish deputies, I drove out on the road and picked out a place to wait for them.

We chose a natural barricade at the top of a little hill, and we secreted ourselves on the side of the road and waited. Alcorn, who personally knew Barrow and Bonnie Parker, sighted their car a quarter of a mile away and told us that was them. When the car got within 100 yards coming up the grade, Alcorn said: "That's them, boys."

About that time the car, which was meeting a truck, slowed down.

---

⁶¹ *Evening star*. (Washington, D.C.) May 24, 1934

We hollered to Barrow to halt as we wished to give them a chance. They went for their guns, and we let them have it.

In the car we found three submachine guns, two automatic sawed off shotguns, four .45-caliber automatic pistols, two .38-caliber automatic pistols and one .45-caliber revolver, also a large quantity of ammunition.[62]

Dorothea Puente

Date	Events
January 9, 1929	Born Dorothea Helen Gray in Redlands, California
1945	Marries Fred McFaul; they have two children – one is put up for adoption, and one is sent to live with relatives. McFaul abandons her in 1948.
Spring 1948	Arrested for passing bad checks; she is sentenced to four months in jail
1952	Marries merchant marine Axel Bren Johansson in San Francisco. Dorothea fritters away his money when he is away at sea.
1960	Arrested for operating a brothel; serves 90-day sentence
1961	Committed to DeWitt State Hospital for various criminal behaviors and suicide attempts; doctors at the hospital diagnose her as a pathological liar with an unstable personality
1966	Gray and Johansson divorce
1968	Marries Roberto Jose Puente; they divorce in 1973
1978	Convicted of illegally cashing thirty-four state and federal checks that belonged to her tenants; she is sentenced to 5 years' probation, and ordered to pay $4,000 in restitution

---

[62] *Evening star.* (Washington, D.C.) May 24, 1934

Date	Events
1982/88	Murders 9 people, mostly for their government checks
November 1988	A social worker reports the disappearance of Alvaro Montoya, who was a tenant in her house; police dig up seven bodies in her yard
1993	Convicted of three of the murders, and sentenced to life without parole
March 27, 2011	Dies in the Central California Women's Facility, Chowchilla, California

Dorothea Puente[63]

She was born Dorothea Helen Gray in Redlands, California on January 9, 1929. In the 1980s, she would murder people in her tenant house, bury them in her yard, and then cash their social security checks. Most of the tenants were elderly or disabled.

---

[63] https://www.youtube.com/watch?v=IMj7T-izZ1M

Her scheme fell apart in November 1988 when a social worker reported the disappearance of Alvaro Montoya, who was a tenant in Puente's house. Police would then dig up seven bodies in her yard.

In 1993, she was convicted of three of the murders, and sentenced to life without parole. She died in the Central California Women's Facility in Chowchilla, California on March 27, 2011.

Below is an article which looks at the victims of Dorothea Puente.

> Victims included Puente's boyfriend Everson Gillmouth, 77, and eight tenants who lived at the boarding house she operated at 1426 F Street in Sacramento: Ruth Munroe, 61; Leona Carpenter, 78; Alvaro "Bert/Alberto" Gonzales Montoya, 51; Dorothy Miller, 64; Benjamin Fink, 55; James Gallop, 62; Vera Faye Martin, 64; and Betty Palmer, 78. The first victim, Munroe, died at 1426 F Street in 1982, but her death was deemed a suicide by drug overdose, although her family suspected Puente was behind her death and pressed for further investigation. Gillmouth's body was found in January 1986 in a wooden box on the bank of the Sacramento River near Verona, just north of Sacramento. The rest of the victims were found buried in Puente's backyard in November 1988 during a police investigation.[64]

Aileen Wuornos

Date	Events
February 29, 1956	Born Aileen Carol Pittman in Rochester, Michigan
March 18, 1960	Legally adopted by her grandparents (both were alcoholics)

---

[64] https://oac.cdlib.org/findaid/ark:/13030/c8b85fn5/

Date	Events
1970	Raped by a friend of her grandfather, Aileen becomes pregnant
March 23, 1971	Has a child who is put up for adoption
May 27, 1974	Arrested in Colorado, for DUI, disorderly conduct, and firing a .22-caliber pistol from a moving vehicle
1976	Marries 69-year old Lewis Gratz Fell. After multiple incidents of Aileen attacking her new husband, he gets a restraining order against her.
July 14, 1976	Arrested in Michigan for assault and disturbing the peace
July 21, 1976	Her marriage with Fell is annulled
August 1976	Arrested for DUI
1978	Attempts suicide
May 20, 1981	Arrested in Edgewater, Florida, for armed robbery of a convenience store
May 1, 1984	Arrested for passing bad checks in Key West
November 30, 1985	Suspect in the theft of a gun and ammunition in Pasco County, Florida
January 4, 1986	Arrested in Miami for car theft, resisting arrest, and obstruction of justice
June 2, 1986	Detained in Volusia County, Florida for allegedly pulling a gun on a man in a car, and demanding $200
1986	Moves in with hotel maid Tyria Moore (in Florida)
July 4, 1987	Aileen and Tyria are questioned by Daytona Police for allegedly attacking someone with a beer bottle
March 12, 1988	Accuses a Daytona Beach bus driver of assault after he throws her off the bus
November 30, 1989	Aileen shoots and kills Richard Charles Mallory, claiming he had tried to rape her

Date	Events
May 19, 1990	Shoots David Andrew Spears, probably in Citrus Country, Florida
May 31, 1990	Shoots and kills Charles Edmund Carskaddon, probably in Pasco County
July 4, 1990	The car of Peter Abraham Siems is found in Orange Springs, Florida. Aileen and Tyria were seen abandoning the car. Siems was never seen again.
July 31, 1990	Shoots and kills Troy Eugene Burress on or about this date, in Marion County, Florida
September 11, 1990	Shoots and kills Charles Richard "Dick" Humphreys, probably in Marion County
November 19, 1990	Shoots and kills Walter Jeno Antonio, probably in Dixie County
January 9, 1991	Arrested on an outstanding warrant in Volusia County
January 16, 1991	Aileen confesses to the murders, but claims they were all in self-defense as the men had tried to rape her
January 27, 1992	Found guilty of the murder of Richard Charles Mallory, partially on the testimony of Tyria Moore
January 31, 1992	Sentenced to death
March 31, 1992	Pleads no contest to the murders of Charles Richard Humphreys, Troy Eugene Burress, and David Andrew Spears. She is given three more death sentences.
June 1992	Pleads guilty to the death of Charles Edmund Carskaddon, and receives another death penalty
1992	Portrayed by Jean Smart in TV-movie *Overkill: The Aileen Wuornos Story*
February 1993	Pleads guilty to the murder of Walter Jeno Antonio, and receives her sixth death sentence

Date	Events
1993	*Aileen Wuornos: The Selling of a Serial Killer* documentary released
1996	U.S. Supreme Court denies her request for an appeal
2001	Petitions the Florida Supreme Court to let her die, for she is guilty of the crimes she was convicted of
October 9, 2002	Executed at Florida State Prison, Raiford, Florida by lethal injection; her remains were cremated
2003	• Portrayed by Charlize Theron (Academy Award) in *Monster* • *Aileen: Life and Death of a Serial Killer* documentary is released

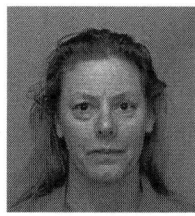

Aileen Wuornos[65]

Aileen Wuornos was born on February 29, 1956 as Aileen Carol Pittman in Rochester, Michigan. She was put to death in 2002 for six murders. She had been murdering her prostitution clients for their money, as she and her girlfriend Tyria Moore needed more money to live.

It is said that she suffered from borderline personality disorder and antisocial personality disorder. She had a long string of criminal charges in several states.

She was executed at Florida State Prison, Raiford, Florida by

---

[65] Florida Department of Corrections, Public Domain.

lethal injection on October 9, 2002. Her remains were cremated.

Andrea Yates

Date	Events
July 2, 1964	Born Andrea Pia Kennedy in Hallsville, Texas
1982	Graduates from Milby High School as valedictorian
1986	Graduates from University of Texas Health Science Center at Houston
1986/1994	Registered nurse
April 17, 1993	Marries Russell "Rusty" Yates; they will have 5 children
June 17, 1999	After the birth of their fourth child, Andrea attempts suicide
July 1999	Nervous breakdown; she attempts suicide twice. Diagnosis: postpartum psychosis.
March 12, 2001	Andrea's father dies
April 1, 2001	Hospitalized after she becomes non-responsive
May 3, 2001	Found in a "near catatonic" state; she had filled the bathtub with water
June 20, 2001	Drowns her five children in a bathtub in their house in Clear Lake City, Texas (a Houston suburb)
March 2002	Found guilty of murder, and sentenced to life imprisonment with eligibility for parole in 40 years
January 6, 2005	Texas appeals court reverses the convictions because of the untrue testimony of an expert witness during the first trial
March 17, 2005	Rusty Yeates granted a divorce
January 9, 2006	Pleads not guilty by reason of insanity

Date	Events
July 26, 2006	Found not guilty by reason of insanity; committed to the North Texas State Hospital–Vernon Campus
January 2007	Moved to Kerrville State Hospital

She was born on July 2, 1964, as Andrea Pia Kennedy in Hallsville, Texas. She became infamous on June 20, 2001 when she drowned her five children in a bathtub in their house in Clear Lake City, Texas (a Houston suburb).

On April 17, 1993, she married Russell "Rusty" Yates. They would have 5 children, even though doctors had warned her to have no more children after her fourth. On June 17, 1999, after the birth of their fourth child, Andrea attempted suicide. A month later, she suffered a nervous breakdown, and twice attempted suicide. The diagnosis was postpartum psychosis.

As noted, on June 20, 2001 she drowned her five children, one at a time, in a bathtub in their house in Clear Lake City, Texas (a Houston suburb). She called the police to report her crime, and then called her husband at work. He had only left her alone for one hour.

In March 2002, she was found guilty of murder, and sentenced to life imprisonment with eligibility for parole in 40 years. On January 6, 2005, a Texas appeals court reversed the convictions because of the untrue testimony of an expert witness during the first trial.

On January 9, 2006, she pleaded not guilty by reason of insanity. The court agreed, and on July 26, 2006, she was found not guilty by reason of insanity and committed to the North Texas State Hospital–Vernon Campus. She was then moved to Kerrville State Hospital in January 2007.

Sources

- *Argus*, The, May 13, 1908
- *Assassination of President Lincoln and the Trial of the Conspirators, The* (Moore, Wilstach and Baldwin, 1865)
- BBC News, October 11, 2005
- *Brownsville Herald*, May 24, 1934
- *Burns Archive, The*
- California Department of Correction
- CASE No. 10., THE BELSEN TRIAL, TRIAL OF JOSEF KRAMER AND 44 OTHERS, BRITISH MILITARY COURT, LUNEBURG, 17TH SEPTEMBER-17TH NOVEMBER, 1945 Part V
- Creative Commons Attribution 4.0 International license, by Reppop.
- *Daily Alaska empire, The*, March 12, 1935
- *Day Book, The* (Chicago, Ill.) August 15, 1913
- *Evening star*, (Washington, D.C.) May 24, 1934
- *Evening star*, October 06, 1945
- *Evening star*. (Washington, D.C.) November 29, 1954
- FBI.
- Florida Department of Corrections
- *Frank Leslie's illustrated newspaper*, v. 76 (June 2, 1893)
- *Guardian, The*, 1890
- *Hartford republican*, The (Hartford, Ky.), November 30, 1894
- *History of the United States Secret Service*, by General L.C. Baker (L.C. Baker, 1867)
- *Imperial War Museum, The*
- *Indianapolis Journal*, Indianapolis, Marion County, June 25, 1902
- Jewish Prisoner Sala Feder on December 1, 1947 to the District Court in Kraków
- Kent County Sheriff's Department
- *Los Angeles Herald*, Volume XXXII, Number 36, November 6, 1904

- *Los Angeles Times*, December 27, 1976, Creative Commons Attribution 4.0 International license.
- Metro Dade Police Department
- National Archives and Records Administration
- *New York Herald*, July 7, 1865
- Photo by the The Goodspeeds
- *Retrospect of Western Travel, Volume 2*, by Harriet Martineau (London: Saunders & Otley, 1838)
- *Strange True Stories of Louisiana* by George W. Cable, Illustrated, 1890
- *The Story of Cole Younger by Himself*, by Cole Younger (Press of the Henneberry Company, 1903)
- Transcript of the Official Shorthand Notes of 'The Trial of Josef Kramer and Forty Four Others'
- United Nations Office on Drugs and Crime. https://sherloc.unodc.org/cld/case-law-doc/drugcrimetype/usa/1988/united_states_v_blanco.html
- United States Holocaust Memorial Museum
- *Washington Star*, 1893.

Links

http://airtreeswateranimals.blogspot.com/p/rainbow.html

http://www.museocriminologico.it/correggio_uk.htm

https://atwaatwar.blog/2011/10/22/red/

https://oac.cdlib.org/findaid/ark:/13030/c8b85fn5/

https://www.youtube.com/watch?v=IMj7T-izZ1M

Library of Congress http://www.loc.gov/pictures/item/2004677307/

Library of Congress https://lccn.loc.gov/2002706295

Library of Congress https://lccn.loc.gov/2016646237

Library of Congress https://lccn.loc.gov/2019632749

Library of Congress. https://lccn.loc.gov/2016652853

www.wikimedia.org
www.wikipedia.org

Front cover:

"A snapshot of criminal Bonnie Parker smoking a cigar, seized by police 4-13-1933" (FBI. Public Domain.) Colorized by the author.

17th century portrait of Elizabeth Bathory (Public Domain.)

"Mugshot taken of Susan Atkins, taken 16 February 2001" (California Department of Corrections. Public Domain.)

The Author on YouTube

There are several extracts of lectures by the author on Civil War topics available on YouTube, including:

Sherman's March: Strategy and Results
(http://www.youtube.com/watch?v=gAcqx0rpWXY)

Sherman's March: The Fall of Savannah
(http://www.youtube.com/watch?v=Iykjb7vA3wI)

Overview of the Great Locomotive Chase
(http://www.youtube.com/watch?v=CSJ03W8mlMc)

Author singing *"Hold the Fort"*
(http://www.youtube.com/watch?v=5LzWtVXAYAE)

Civil War Quick Note: Clara Barton
(http://youtu.be/7Td0lu49hsw)

A Brief Look at Patrick Cleburne
(http://youtu.be/qagsf7uUgZo)

A Brief Look at "Bloody Bill" Anderson
(http://youtu.be/Y-vA6BKaOWA)

All of these can be viewed in high definition (720p).

The author is available for lectures in Georgia, Alabama, southern Tennessee, eastern Kansas and southeastern Pennsylvania.

For details, see: http://www.rcjbooks.com/guest_speaker.

About the Author

Robert C. Jones served as President of the Kennesaw Historical Society for 21 years (1994-2015), and also served as a member of the executive board of the Kennesaw Museum Foundation for 17 years (1998-2015). The Museum Foundation helped fund the 45,000 square foot Southern Museum of Civil War and Locomotive History in Kennesaw, GA. He has written several books on the Civil War, the American Revolution, and other historical themes, including:

- A Guide to the Civil War in Alabama
- A Guide to the Civil War in Georgia
- Americans Walk on the Moon – the Road to Apollo 11
- Battle of Allatoona Pass: The Forgotten Battle of Sherman's Atlanta Campaign, The
- Battle of Chickamauga: A Brief History, The
- Battle of Griswoldville: An Infantry Battle on Sherman's March to the Sea, The
- Bleeding Kansas: The Real Start of the Civil War
- Civil War Prison Camps: A Brief History
- Colonial Georgia: 1733 - 1800
- Confederate Invasion of New Mexico, The
- Conspirators, Assassins, and the Death of Abraham Lincoln
- The End of the Civil War: 1865
- The End of the Civil War in Georgia: 1865
- Famous Songs of the Civil War
- Fifteen Most Critical Moments of the Civil War, The
- George Washington and the Continental Army: 1777/1778
- Great Naval Battles of the Civil War
- Heroes and Heroines of the American Revolution
- Hitler's Wonder Weapons
- Lost Confederate Gold
- McCook's Raid and the Battle of Brown's Mill
- Pennsylvania Railroad: An Illustrated Timeline, The
- Reading Railroad: An Illustrated Timeline, The
- Retracing the Route of Sherman's Atlanta Campaign (expanded edition)
- Retracing the Route of Sherman's March to the Sea (expanded edition)
- Top 10 Reasons Why the Civil War Was Won in the

- West, The
- Ten Best – and Worst – Generals of the Civil War, The
- Top 20 Civil War Spies and Secret Agents, The
- Top 20 Railroad Songs of All Time, The
- Top 25 Most Influential Women of the Civil War, The
- Top Innovations of World War I
- Top Innovations of World War II
- W&A, the General, and the Andrews Raid: A Brief History, The
- The War of 1812: A Brief History
- Witchcraft in Colonial America
- Women who Murder

Robert C. Jones is an ordained elder in the Presbyterian Church. He has written and taught numerous adult Sunday School courses. He is also the author of a number of books on Christian history and theology topics. For a list, see http://rcjbooks.com/christian_history.

Robert has also written several books on "Old West" themes, including:

- A Guide to Frontier Kansas
- Death Valley Ghost Towns – As They Appear Today
- Famous Women of the Old West
- Ghost Towns, Forts and Pueblos of New Mexico (expanded edition)
- Ghost Towns of Southern Arizona and New Mexico
- Ghost Towns of the Mojave National Preserve
- Ghost Towns of Western Nevada
- Top 10 Gunslingers and Lawmen of the Old West, The

In 2005, Robert co-authored a business-oriented book entitled *Working Virtually: The Challenges of Virtual Teams*.

Also in 2013, Robert published *The Leo Beuerman Story: As Told by his Family*.

In 2014, Robert published *Ghost Towns and Mills of the Atlanta Area*.

http://www.rcjbooks.com/ jone442@bellsouth.net

Made in the USA
Columbia, SC
17 February 2023